LET'S MEET FAMOUS COMPOSERS

A Creative Music Activity Book

By

Harriet Kinghorn
Jacqueline Badman
Lisa Lewis-Spicer

Illustrated by
Margherita DePaulis

Publishers
T.S. Denison & Company, Inc.,
Minneapolis, Minnesota

T.S. Denison & Co., Inc.

No part of this publication may be reproduced or transmitted by any means, mechanical or electronic, including photocopying or recording, or stored in any information storage or retrieval system without permission from the publisher. Reproducible pages may be duplicated by the classroom teacher for use in the classroom, but not for commercial sale. Reproduction for an entire school or school system is strictly prohibited.

Standard Book Number: 513-02101-9
Let's Meet Famous Composers
Copyright © 1992 by the T.S. Denison & Co., Inc.
Minneapolis, Minnesota 55431

INTRODUCTION

Our hope in writing *Let's Meet Famous Composers* is to share with each reader information about the colorful lives of some composers who have so enormously contributed to our world. In the following biographies and accompanying activities and evaluation, and in the glossary and bibliography, a teacher may reproduce for students those pages pertinent to the course of study. For those invaluable teachers working at home—parents—one may read with their children to discover more about our world of music.

We encourage all students and adults alike to learn about and appreciate musicians and composers who enrich our lives so fully. If we nurture in each child an awareness and appreciation of fine music, future generations may be encouraged to create their own Beethovens and Bernsteins. These future musicians and composers may emerge from your very own classroom or home!

> Harriet Kinghorn
> Jacqueline Badman
> Lisa Lewis-Spicer

Table of Contents

SUGGESTIONS FOR PARENTS AND TEACHERS

1. Read the included biography to obtain background information on a specific composer. (For school use, the biography section may be reproduced and stapled along with the corresponding activity sheet to make a booklet on each composer.) You may wish to consult the bibliography in the back of this book for further information.

2. After reading biographic information on a composer, complete the corresponding project suggested on the activity sheet or a similar project of your own choosing. The majority of the evaluation questions following the activity pages are open-ended and may be answered independent of the project indicated.

3. After responding to the questions on the evaluation sheet, share and discuss the various responses in a group setting.

4. While studying the composers and listening to their work, children should be reminded that composers not only create music for its beautiful sounds, but as with any other art form, music may be the result of individual expression, an emotional release, or a learning experience.

Name: _____

BACKGROUND INFORMATION

Composer: _____

ABOUT A COMPOSER

Find at least three sources that contain information about the composer. Sources might include encyclopedias, books, filmstrips, newspapers, magazines, or other reference materials.

Title of Source:	Pages on which information was found:

INFORMATION DISCOVERED ABOUT THIS COMPOSER

_____
_____
_____
_____
_____
_____
_____
_____
_____
_____
_____
_____

Johann Sebastian Bach
(bahkh)
1685–1750

Johann Sebastian Bach was born on March 21, 1685, into a large family of musicians in the town of Eisenach, Germany. For many years the Bach family—uncles, aunts, cousins, brothers, and sisters—had sung and played musical instruments. Since Johann Sebastian's father was the town organist and a court musician, it was natural for him to teach his young son to play the violin. Johann Sebastian played often and eagerly looked forward to the Bach family's annual reunion and musical festival where all the Bachs gathered to produce beautiful music.

The town of Eisenach was very proud of its fine choir boys who sang during church masses and wedding celebrations. Young Johann Sebastian eventually became one of these choir boys and was renowned for his beautiful soprano voice. When he was only ten years old, Johann Sebastian's mother and father died. The young boy was sent to live with his older brother, Johann Christoph, who was an organist in the town of Ohrdruf. While attending school, Johann Sebastian took lessons from his brother on the clavier, a small keyboard instrument similar to a piano. Young Johann Sebastian was eager to learn all that he could, but his older brother, Johann Christoph, thought that Johann Sebastian was moving too quickly throught his lessons and that some of the music was too difficult for him to master.

One day, Johann Sebastian saw his brother bring home a large book of church music. Desperate to learn material, Johann Sebastian begged his brother to teach him the music. But Johann Christoph thought the pieces were much too difficult for his younger brother. Fortunately, Johann Sebastian saw where Johann Christoph carefully placed the precious music. When everyone was asleep and all was quiet, Johann Sebastian tiptoed downstairs and removed the book from its cupboard. When he reached his bedroom, Johann Sebastian began to copy, by the light of the moon, each note of music into his own notebook. When he could write no longer and his fingers were numb, Johann Sebastian carefully returned the book of music.

Night after night, whenever the moon shone brightly, Johann Sebastian worked hard copying the music. Often times, his brother wondered why Johann

Sebastian was so sleepy in the mornings! But Johann Sebastian kept his secret and finally, six months later when all the music was written down, Johann Sebastian eagerly ran to the clavier and played endlessly. Whenever Johann Christoph left the house, Johann Sebastian played the music his brother had thought too difficult for him. Even when Johann Christoph finally discovered his little brother playing the stolen music, he *still* thought the music was too difficult for Johann Sebastian!

When he was fifteen years old, Johann Sebastian had to leave his brother's crowded household. Johann Sebastian walked two hundred miles to Lüneberg to attend St. Michael's School where he sang in the choir in exchange for his room and board. He also continued to study the violin and clavier while also learning to play the harpsichord. But it was the organ, the queen of instruments, which captured Johann Sebastian's musical soul. Johann Sebastian traveled many miles, often on foot, to listen to and study with master organists, including Reinken and Buxtehude.

When he was eighteen years old, Johann Sebastian obtained a position as organist and choir-master at a new church in Arnstadt; it was then that he pledged to write music in honor of God alone. Johann Sebastian did not want worldly fame—he only wanted to compose and play music "in the name of the Lord" and in fact, at the top of all his music bore the heading "in the name of the Lord" or "to the glory of God alone."

Johann Sebastian left his position in Arnstadt to become a music master in Mülhausen where the people of that parish promised him more time to compose. Here, Johann Sebastian was married and he and his young wife, Maria Bach, eventually had seven children, three of whom became famous composers.

From Mülhausen, Bach moved to Weimar where he worked happily for nine years under the Duke of Weimar, a deeply religious man. In 1717, his fame as a composer and organist renowned throughout Germany, Bach was asked by Prince Leopold of Köthen to be his court organist and orchestra master.

A large portion of Bach's compositions was religious music, including many cantatas for the church. He also wrote many suites for the clavichord and harpsichord and many fugues for the organ and piano. From his studies of Italian instrumental music, particularly the work of the Italian composer Antonio Vivaldi, Bach was prompted to write many concertos and sonatas, including the six *Brandenburg Concertos*. Additionally, he wrote *The Well-Tempered Clavier*, a collection of compositions for the instruction and appreciation of music.

In 1720, Bach's wife died and a year later he married Anna Magdalena, the daughter of a court trumpeter who much inspired his work. Three years later, Bach and his family moved to Leipzig where he was the music director at the St. Thomas School. Despite all his teaching and family responsibilities (he eventually had twenty children, many of whom became musicians) Bach continued to write one masterpiece after another—the *Christmas* Oratorio, the *Goldberg Variations*, and his last monumental work, *The Art of the Fugue*.

The many years of overstraining his eyes in poor light while writing and copying music took its toll in 1749 when Bach became totally blind. A year later, Bach died of a stroke. Because Bach spent most of his life in one area of Germany, little of his music was known throughout the world. It wasn't until nearly one hundred years later when two composers, Felix Mendelssohn and Robert Schumann, rediscovered the wonders of his music and shared them with the world. The famous eighteenth century composer Wolfgang Amadeus Mozart once declared Johann Sebastian Bach "the father of all music."

Activity Sheet   Name _____

Johann Sebastian Bach

MATERIALS: Portrait of Johann Sebastian Bach (above), white construction paper, crayons or markers, scissors, glue, writing paper, and pencil.

ACTIVITY:

1. Find and read as much information about Johann Sebastian Bach as possible.

2. Cut out the picture above or draw your own portrait of Bach.

3. Glue Bach's portrait in the center of a piece of drawing paper. Then draw and color objects and scenes around the protrait that you associate with the life of Bach.

4. On a separate sheet of paper, write about Bach's life. Include some information about each of the objects or scenes that you have illustrated on your paper.

5. Glue the information you have written to the back of your drawing.

Evaluation　　　　　　　　　　　Name_____

THINKING ABOUT BACH AND ME

Respond to four or more of the following questions/statements:

1. What did Bach enjoy doing most when he was a boy?

2. Compare an organ to a piano. How is an organ similar to a piano? How is it different?

3. List three of Bach's compositions you have heard. Underline the one you like most. Explain why it is your favorite composition.

4. If you could meet Bach today, what three (or more) questions would you ask him?

5. List at least five things that you think Bach missed seeing after he became blind.

6. Write one or more paragraphs about what you have learned about this composer and/or what you have learned through your activity relating to his composer.

Ludwig van Beethoven
(bay-toe-vehn)
1770–1827

Ludwig van Beethoven—along with Franz Joseph Haydn and Wolfgang Amadeus Mozart—was one of the greatest classical composers. The classical period of music occurred between the years 1750 to 1825. The hallmarks of this period of music were balance and order; the music was carefully defined and arranged and broke away from the highly complex and ornamented music of the baroque period, when the composers Johann Sebastian Bach and George Frederic Handel reigned. Beethoven revolutionized the form and spirit of music during the classical period, becoming the first composer to earn a living from the sale of his compositions. He was an independent and spirited man and at a time when composers were regarded as servants of the aristocracy, Beethoven considered himself one of their members. Although highly irregular for the time, the aristocracy respected Beethoven and treated him as an equal. As a result of his prestige, Beethoven was fortunate to be able to write only those compositions he wanted to write, rather than compositions an archbishop or king ordered him to create. Beethoven became the forerunner of the music of the romantic period when new, rich, and colorful musical forms began to emerge.

Ludwig van Beethoven was born in Bonn, a city on the Rhine River in Germany, on December 16, 1770. His father and grandfather were both professional musicians and Ludwig's father, Johann van Beethoven, was eager for his son to become like Mozart—another musical genius whose expertise was evident at a very young age. When he was only four years old Ludwig's father began instructing him. Every day Ludwig studied violin, piano, and composition. Then when he was nine years old, a musician friend of this father's, Tobias Pfeiffer, became his teacher. Often times, after spending all night at an ale house, Ludwig's father and Herr Pfeiffer would return home and rouse Ludwig from his sleep to give him music lessons, no matter what time of the night it was!

When Ludwig was about twelve years old, he began to study the *Forty–Eight Preludes and Fugues* of Johann Sebastian Bach, a famous German baroque composer and organist. Ludwig found great inspiration in Bach's preludes and fugues. In 1782, a year after his first published composition, Beethoven obtained a paid position as a second court organist.

At the age of seventeen, Beethoven visited Vienna, a city famous for musical activity, and where eight years later he would eventually give his first public performance. While on this first visit to Vienna, Beethoven had the opportunity to play for Mozart, who was very impressed by Beethoven's ability to improvise— or to make up music on the spur of the moment. Of Beethoven's performance, Mozart supposedly said, "Someday he will give the world something worth listening to."

Shortly after visiting Vienna, Beethoven's mother died and in order to care for his younger brothers and sister, Beethoven began to give piano lessons. One of the families he met through his instruction were the von Breunings, a wealthy and intellectual family. Frau von Breuning, the mother of one of Beethoven's piano students, introduced Beethoven to the works of Shakespere and the German poet, Goethe. Beethoven was immensely grateful to the von Breunings for introducing him to this new world of literature and learning.

One day the famous composer Joseph Haydn came to Bonn and Beethoven had the opportunity to play for him. The Archbishop of Bonn, who hired Beethoven as an organist in 1784, arranged for Beethoven to study under Haydn in Vienna.

After he completed his studies with Haydn, Beethoven decided to settle in Vienna and to diligently pursue composing and performing. His first public concert, given in Vienna in 1795 when he was twenty-five years old, earned him enormous praise. Beethoven became the first great composer to work without the aid of a wealthy benefactor. His independence made it difficult for him to serve one family; he felt he performed and expressed himself best when serving the public.

Beethoven's greatest productivity occurred between the years 1795 and 1815. He composed eight of his nine symphonies; twenty-seven of this thirty-two sonatas for piano and violin; eleven of his sixteen quartets; his only opera, *Fidelio*; and several masses. Sadly, at the time of his last public concert for the Vienna Congress in 1815, Beethoven was nearly deaf, and by 1820 he could no longer conduct his orchestra. Musical expression was vital to Beethoven's existence, and he courageously continued to compose music whose sounds he could only hear in his own mind. Some of his greatest compositions were produced when he was completely deaf.

Beethoven died on March 26, 1827, from complications of pneumonia. His immortal nine symphonies are often considered his greatest works. His *Ninth Symphony* contains the great choral section *Ode to Joy*, and together with the *Fifth Symphony*, these works remain his most popular. The third symphony, *Eroica*, is said to have been Beethoven's favorite.

Activity Sheet   Name _____

Ludwig van Beethoven

MATERIALS: 5" x 7" index card, pencils, colored crayons or markers.

ACTIVITY:

1. Pretend you are in Germany and you have just attended the annual Beethoven Festival.

2. You will make a postcard to send home.

3. Using your colored crayons or markers, decorate the front of the postcard. Design something that relates to the Beethoven Festival.

4. On the back of the postcard, write about what you have done, the music you have heard, and the sights you have seen.

Evaluation   Name _____

THINKING ABOUT BEETHOVEN AND ME

Respond to four or more of the following questions/statements:

1. Beethoven was grateful to many people who had helped him over the years. Name one of these people and tell how you think he/she helped Beethoven.

2. After listening to some of Beethoven's music, write the name of your favorite composition and tell why you like it most.

3. What helped Beethoven cope with his deafness? How would you try to cope if you became deaf? List at least five things that you would not be able to enjoy if you were deaf.

4. Name five different musical forms that Beethoven wrote during his lifetime.

5. Briefly describe the postcard that you designed. To whom will you send it?

6. Write one or more paragraphs about what you have learned about this composer and/or what you have learned through your own creative artwork relating to this composer.

Leonard Bernstein
1918–1990

Leonard Bernstein was unlike many other composers who began their musical studies at an early age. It was not until he was ten years old that Lenny (as all his family members called him) began piano lessons after his Aunt Clara moved her large piano to the Bernstein family apartment. It was no easy task for young Lenny to convince his nonmusical parents to allow him to take lessons. Lenny's father, Sam Bernstein, was a successful barbershop supplies salesman who wanted Lenny to help him in the business when he was older. But once Lenny set eyes on Aunt Clara's piano, he fell in love with it and knew he wanted to be a musician when he grew up. As an adult, Leonard Bernstein became a great musician and the first American to become a famous symphony conductor. Remarkable in many ways, Leonard Bernstein is best known for his great achievements as conductor, composer, and pianist.

The son of Russian immigrants, Leonard Bernstein was born in Lawrence, Massachusetts, on August 25, 1918. His father wanted Lenny to help him in his business, and he did not understand why Lenny would want to be a musician. After much begging and pleading, Lenny was finally allowed to take piano lessons. He was a quick learner and was soon reading notes. His piano teacher, Helen Coates (who many years later became his personal secretary), made him practice regularly. Everyone told the Bernsteins that their son was a born musician.

When Lenny graduated from the Boston Latin School he was one of the top ten students in his high school class. Although he excelled in all his studies, music was where his heart lay. After high school, Lenny attended Harvard University where in 1939 he graduated with honors in music. His interest in conducting blossomed when he met Dimitri Metropoulous, a famous European conductor, who suggested Lenny become a conductor too. When Lenny enrolled at the Curtis Institute of Music in Philadelphia, he studied piano, composing, and conducting. Lenny's conducting teacher, Fritz Reiner, thought Lenny was his most gifted student.

At the music school Tanglewood, where Lenny studied during the summer, he met many influential musicians. He studied with the famous conductor Serge Koussevitzky, was inspired by the composer Aaron Copland; and was invited by

Arthur Rodzinski, the conductor of the New York Philharmonic Symphony Orchestra, to come and be his assistant. At the age of twenty-five, Leonard Bernstein was the assistant conductor of the largest orchestra in the United States.

In 1943, Bruno Walter was invited to be the guest conductor of the New York Philharmonic. When it came time for the performance he became ill and the conductor, Arthur Rodzinski, was out of town. On short notice, Lenny was asked to take the conductor's place. The concert was broadcast nationally and Lenny was nervous, but as soon as he looked at the score he regained his composure and threw himself wholeheartedly into conducting the orchestra. The audience members enjoyed watching Lenny conduct almost as much as they enjoyed hearing the orchestra. Not only did his hand move to guide the musicians, but his head rolled, his shoulders shook, and his feet stomped as if to punctuate every beat of the music. He later became well-known for his pirouettes at the podium. So great was the reaction of the audience to the performance, Leonard Bernstein became famous overnight.

From 1958 to 1969, Bernstein served as the musical director of the New York Philharmonic. Under his leadership, the orchestra's prestige and the audience attendance grew rapidly. Bernstein became popular with both children and adults as he eagerly shared his passion for learning and loving music. Often he performed as a solo pianist with the orchestra. He was invited to conduct great orchestras all over the world and was the first American-trained conductor invited to La Scala in Milan, Italy, the most famous opera house in the world. He wrote a great variety of music for all tastes: musicals (*On the Town*, 1944; *Wonderful Town*, 1953; *West Side Story*, 1957), symphonies (*Jeremiah*, 1944), ballets (*Fancy Free*, 1944), a short opera (*Trouble in Tahiti*, 1952), a motion picture score (*On the Waterfront*, 1594), and a long jazz composition entitled "*Prelude, Fugue, and Riffs*."

In 1969, Bernstein no longer wished to be maestro of the Philharmonic, but wanted to pursue other avenues related to music. He became the Philharmonic's guest conductor, still dazzling and delighting his audience with his conducting (and his singing—at rehearsals and concerts he often loudly and jubilantly sang every note of the music). Bernstein went on to direct television and recording programs, to teach and write books about music, and to continue playing the piano.

On Sunday, October 14th, 1990; Bernstein, the recipient of much praise and many awards—including Grammys, Emmys, and a Tony—died of lung failure in his Manhattan apartment. The world still revels in the amazing talents of Leonard Bernstein—composer, conductor, and pianist.

Leonard Bernstein

MATERIALS: "Conducting Techniques" Activity Sheet on the following page, removable tape to hold paper in shape of baton, and a recording of Leonard Bernstein's music.

ACTIVITIES:

1. Study the conducting techniques of a conductor on the following page.

2. Roll up the activity sheet and tape it to represent a baton.

3. Listen to Leonard Bernstein's music as you conduct with your paper baton.

Activity Sheet   Name _____

Leonard Bernstein—Conducting Techniques

A conductor controls an orchestra. The conductor must make sure that the instruments are being played in time with each other and that no instrument overshadows any of the other instruments (unless it is supposed to).

With one hand the conductor uses a baton to indicate the number of beats and the tempo. With the other hand, the conductor gives the musicians musical cues and tells them how the music should be played (quietly, loudly, slowly, quickly).

2 beats in a bar.   3 beats in a bar.   4 beats in a bar.

Quiet   Loud   Giving a cue

Evaluation   Name _____

THINKING ABOUT BERNSTEIN AND ME

Respond to four or more of the following questions/statements:

1. Make a list of the various kinds of instruments that can be found in an orchestra.

2. Write a paragraph to briefly describe the New York Philharmonic Orchestra.

3. Study the responsibilities of a conductor. What do you think you would like the best and least about being a conductor?

4. Find and list the names of at least six pieces that Bernstein composed.

5. You have just returned home from a concert directed by Leonard Bernstein. Write in your journal about your experience at the concert.

6. Write one or more paragraphs about what you have learned about this composer and/or what you have learned through your activity project relating to this composer.

Johannes Brahms
(brahmz)
1833–1897

Johannes Brahms was a German romantic composer of intensely emotional and sentimental symphonies, concertos, and chamber music. He was also one of the greatest creators of *lieder*, German art songs. Brahms was very patient and worked endlessly on his compositions. Brahms spent ten years working intermittently on his first symphony. When it was finally published it caused a great sensation in the music world. Because Brahms was a perfectionist, very little of his "bad" music survives—he immediately destroyed anything that did not meet his standards.

Johannes Brahms was born in Hamburg, Germany—the birthplace of Felix Mendelssohn, another famous romantic composer—on May 7, 1833. Johannes' father was a double bass player who taught his son the elements of music at the age of six. Johannes' father had planned to train his son as an orchestra musician, like himself, but when Johannes began to study the piano, his father recognized his exceptional talent as a pianist.

As a result of the rapid progress in his piano studies, Johannes was recommended to Eduard Marxsen, a wise and sensible instructor who protected Johannes from others seeking to exploit what they perceived as a child prodigy.

When he was thirteen years old, Johannes had to help his relatively poor parents with the family income. He earned his living by playing the piano in dockside taverns on the Hamburg waterfront. Johannes continued to play the piano for dances and in taverns for several years. In addition, he also gave music lessons and appeared in concerts. When he was seventeen years old he met the famous Hungarian violinist, Reményi, whom he accompanied on a tour of Germany in 1853. Reményi and another famous violinist, Joseph Joachim, whom Johannes met while touring, both encouraged Johannes' musical development. Joachim, very much impressed with Johannes, helped his career by giving him a letter of introduction to Robert Schumann, a German composer and renowned pianist. Johannes' talent inspired Schumann to write an article in the *New Music Journal*. Thanks to Schumann's praise and encouragement, some of Johannes Brahms' music was published in Leipzig, Germany. And so, in 1853 Brahms began a deep and lasting friendship with Robert Schumann and his wife,

Clara, a famous pianist as well. Even after Schumann's unfortunate death in 1856, Brahms remained a devoted friend to Clara Schumann.

Brahms had secured an important place for himself in the musical world. He moved to Vienna, Austria, settled there permanently, and became the conductor of the music school, *Singakademie*. Later he gave up the position to devote all of his time to composing. Brahms began working on the outstanding choral work, *German Requiem*. This work is based on passages from the German Bible and was performed for the first time at the Bremen Cathedral in 1868. At this time Brahms was also the artistic director of the *Gesellschaft der Musik freunde*, or Society of the Friends of Music. Most of Brahms' great music was written later in his life. He was forty-three years old when his first symphony was completed; together with his other three symphonies completed in 1877, 1883, and 1885, these have remained standard works for every symphony opera. Each symphony is completely different in its harmonious appeal.

Although Johannes Brahms never married, many speculated he was in love with Clara Schumann. When Brahms learned of Clara's death in 1896, he hurried to Frankfurt, Germany, to attend her funeral. Anxious and angry because he had trouble in catching his train, Brahms became very ill. He believed that his burst of anger at missing his train had ruined his health. Nevertheless, he never recovered from his illness and he died in Vienna on April 3, 1897.

Johannes Brahms

MATERIALS: Yourself, a partner (optional), a spacious room.

ACTIVITY:

1. Brahms wrote a variety of rich, colorful, and textured music.

2. Choose two of Brahms' musical selections that are different from one another.

3. You are a robot that is fueled by Brahms' music. Act out what you hear and describe it in your movement. Is your movement fast, slow, wild, gentle, or fluid? Make the movement based on what you hear and what feels right to you.

4. By choosing two songs, you allow yourself a variety of movement.

Evaluation   Name _____

THINKING ABOUT BRAHMS AND ME

Respond to four or more of the following questions/statements:

1. What musical selections did you choose? Describe your movement to the music.

2. Describe how you would feel if there were no music. How would your life be different? Describe how the Brahms' activity would be different.

3. When Brahms was taking piano lessons at age seven, he enjoyed it so much that he would study nearly all day long. Have you ever had, or do you have, a lesson or subject that you studied or could study all day long?

4. Brahms' career could have been furthered by associating with a famous musician named Franz Liszt. Brahms, however, did not like Liszt or his friends and did not receive any help from Liszt. Do you think Brahms should have pretended to like Liszt so he could receive help in his career, or do you think he made the right decision? Explain.

5. Brahms met someone who was famous and very likeable. His friend, Robert Schumann, was helpful in the development of Brahms' musical career. Has anyone ever helped you to achieve something? Describe how this person helped you.

6. Write one or more paragraphs about what you have learned about this composer and/or what you have learned through your activity project relating to this composer.

Frédéric François Chopin
(sho-pan)
1810-1849

In a small Polish village, not far from Warsaw, Frédéric François Chopin was born on February 22, 1810. His French father, who played the violin and flute; and his Polish mother, who played the piano, nurtured his love for music. When Chopin was six years old, he began to take music lessons—his ability to play the piano and improvise astounded all who heard him.

From the time of his birth, Chopin was surrounded by music. His older sister often helped Chopin at the piano and Chopin's parents quickly realized his unusual and advanced skills. Chopin had a vivid imagination and besides playing works by Bach and Mozart, he created his own compositions. When Chopin was only seven years old, he was giving recitals in private homes and when he was nine years old, he performed a piano concerto for a public audience. Several years later, Chopin entered the Warsaw Conservatory and studied under a teacher named Josef Elsner. The young student's skill and technique were obvious to Elsner and he encouraged Chopin's abilities.

Chopin eventually traveled to Berlin, Vienna, Prague, and Dresden where he played in small concerts with great success. He disliked playing in large concert halls and much preferred the intimacy of small drawing rooms.

Chopin's 1829 concert debut was enthusiastically received. A year later, Chopin left Warsaw again, never to return. A group of his close friends, bidding Chopin farewell, presented him with a going away gift—a silver goblet filled with Polish earth. It was a gift Chopin treasured to the end of his life. Chopin often grieved for his homeland as Poland was seeking to free itself from the oppressive rule of Russia. Chopin composed the *Revolutionary Etude* in response to his despair. Chopin was later to give a concert tour in England and Scotland in order to raise money for the increasing number of Polish refugees. While Chopin spent most of the remainder of his life in Paris, then the world center of art and culture, his love of Poland was always foremost on his mind.

Chopin had set out for Paris in 1831 in order to make a name for himself. He was still a young, impressionable man, twenty-one years old. His first concert in Paris was such a phenomenal success that Chopin did not continue on to London as he initially intended. Instead, after that concert, Chopin agreed to instruct several students eager to study with him. His fame became renowned throughout the city of Paris where he was admitted into the exclusive inner circles of other musicians and artists. Chopin's work delighted composers such as the Hungarian composer Franz Liszt, who was to become Chopin's good friend, and the German composer Felix Mendelssohn. The French poets Victor Hugo and Balzac were great admirers of Chopin as was Eugéne Delacroix, the French painter. During this time in Paris, Chopin was most happy and productive; although he was a perfectionist who worked very slowly, he composed many nocturnes, études, waltzes, ballads, mazurkas, and polonaises. Among his works at this time was the famous *Minute Waltz*. His graceful playing and delicate technique often moved his audience to tears.

In 1837, when Chopin was twenty-seven years old, his friend Franz Liszt introduced him to the famous novelist George Sand. George Sand was a woman, an energetic and tempermental writer, who had taken a man's name because women writers during the early nineteenth century were seldom acknowledged. Chopin and George Sand fell deeply in love.

Chopin was an elegant man but he was also very frail. George Sand encouraged him to go to Majorca, an island south of Spain, where Chopin could regain his strength. Chopin agreed and even had his piano shipped from Paris to Majorca. But the weather that winter in Majorca was damp and cold which only worsened Chopin's condition. Chopin caught a bad cold and became very ill; the medical doctors diagnosed him as having an incurable lung disease called tuberculosis.

Chopin captured his feelings of despair and hopelessness in his *Prelude in D Flat Major*. While George Sand nursed him night and day, Chopin longed to return to the elegance and gaiety of Paris. After their return to Paris, Chopin and Sand ended their relationship.

During the last few years of his life, Chopin devoted his energies to raising money for Poland. His concert fund-raising was exhausting and on October 17, 1849, sick and depressed, Chopin died in Paris surrounded by his close friends. Chopin's own *Funeral March* was played at his funeral and when he was buried, the Polish earth that had been presented to him in the silver cup was scattered over his grave.

Being a romanticist, Chopin wrote directly from his emotions. His music clearly expressed his thoughts and feelings. When he brooded over the destruction of Poland, his music was sad; occasionally his music was gay and lively, perhaps reflecting his happy years in Paris. Chopin treated the piano as a solo instrument—his innovations in fingering and pedaling gave the sounds of the piano new, exciting potential.

Name _____

Frédéric François Chopin

MATERIALS: Drawing paper; colored chalk, crayons, or markers; and a Chopin recording.

ACTIVITY:

1. Frédéric Chopin was a very expressive pianist. His moods were reflected in his music.

2. You will use Chopin's music to express yourself. Gather your drawing materials on a desk or table. While you are listening to a Chopin musical recording, compose a drawing that reflects what you are hearing and feeling in the music. Are you, for example, seeing bright colors and lively movement, or are you seeing dark images and stormy surroundings?

Name_____

THINKING ABOUT CHOPIN AND ME

Respond to four or more of the following questions/statements:

1. Explain the similarities between Mozart's and Chopin's childhoods.

2. Even though Chopin left Poland, explain how he remained loyal to his homeland with his music.

3. During his lifetime, Chopin visited the cities of Berlin, Vienna, Prague, Dresden, and Paris. Tell which countries each of these cities are located in.

4. If you chose to draw along with the music, describe your drawing and tell how it was inspired by Chopin's music. Name the title of the song you worked on.

5. Chopin traveled extensively and died far away from home. Would you want to travel to the countries that Chopin did? Would you like to live in a country other than the one you were born in? Explain your answers.

6. Write one or more paragraphs about what you have learned about this composer and/or what you have learned through your activity project relating to this composer.

Edward "Duke" Ellington
1899-1974

Edward Kennedy "Duke" Ellington was the most famous jazz composer of the 1900s. He was the composer of such famous works as "Satin Doll," "Sophisticated Lady," "Creole Love Call," and "Do Nothin' Till You Hear From Me." He was also known as a great band leader and pianist.

Born in Washington D.C., on April 19, 1899, Ellington began to study the piano when he was seven years old. When he was a little older, he began playing in local orchestras. In 1923, Ellington formed the group "Washingtonians" and two years later he made his first record. The Washingtonians became one of the most important big bands in America. Through developing their own unique sounds and new and unusual arrangements, Ellington and his band became well-known and increasingly famous while performing at the Cotton Club in Harlem (New York City) from 1927 to 1932.

During the 1930s, Ellington and his group made a series of concert tours throughout the United States and Europe. Ellington's fame as a songwriter increased and he began to write the first of his longer compositions including "Creole Rhapsody" and "Reminiscing In Tempo."

Ellington's greatest talent may have been his ability to surround himself with the best musicians and soloists available. He composed many works to highlight the unique talent of soloists like Barney Bigard (clarinetist), Harry Carney and Johnny Hodges (saxophonists), and Cootie Williams (trumpeter). Ellington gave his soloists generous space to exercise their creative energies through improvisation—composing as one plays. This on-the-spot composing ability is vital to jazz music, and the improvisations in Ellington's band were among the most electrifying. Because of the artistic freedom allowed them and Ellington's good nature, nearly all of Ellington's players stayed with him. The balance between the orchestra and the improvisation of each soloist was so outstanding, Ellington was able to develop orchestral suites like *Black, Brown, And Beige*, one of his most famous suites. The *Black, Brown, And Beige Suite* of 1943 was first performed at a concert in Carnegie Hall in New York City where Ellington introduced a new composition every year from 1943 to 1950.

During the early 1940s, Billy Strayhorn, who had become Ellington's collaborator in composing and arranging music, and bassist Jimmy Blanton made important contributions to the band which further increased the band's already widespread appeal.

After 1956, Ellington composed a wide variety of music including several suites, musical scores for motion pictures, religious music, and a Black history pageant called *My People*. He wrote a total of over nine hundred compositions in his lifetime.

Duke Ellington, one of the leading figures in jazz history, developed a great rapport between his band and the audience for whom they performed. Ellington realized that one of the most important elements of jazz—America's music—was the love of playing happy, vivacious music. Ellington and his band produced these new, exciting rhythms like no one had before.

Activity Sheet   Name _____

Duke Ellington

MATERIALS: Paint, markers or crayons, tagboard or large sheets of paper.

ACTIVITY:

1. When Edward "Duke" Ellington was a young man, he painted signs during the day and often played in a band at night to make a living. Now, it is your turn to make a sign for Duke Ellington.

2. Design a sign to advertise one of Duke Ellington's jazz concerts in a city of your choice. Remember to tell when and where this concert will be presented, and if there will be an admission fee.

3. After your sign is completed, listen to music by Duke Ellington's band. Pretend you are at the concert for which you designed the sign.

Evaluation   Name _____

THINKING ABOUT DUKE ELLINGTON AND ME

1. If you were a professional musician in Duke Ellington's band, what instrument would you like to play? Why?

2. You are attending a reception for Duke Ellington. Write what you see, hear, taste, smell, touch, and do at this reception.

3. Nearly all of Duke Ellington's band players stayed with his band. Describe how you think Duke Ellington treated his band members to make them want to stay with him.

4. Explain what you think were some of the advantages and disadvantages that Duke Ellington encountered as he traveled from one place to another on his band tours.

5. If you could talk to Duke Ellington, what three questions would you ask him?

6. Write one or more paragraphs about what you have learned about this composer and/or what you have learned through your activity project relating to this composer.

George Gershwin
1898-1937

Morris and Rose Gershwin, newly arrived immigrants from Russia, became the proud parents of George Gershwin on September 26, 1898, in Brooklyn, New York. Little did they know that their son would musically capture the soul of an entire nation.

Young George grew up on the sidewalks of New York where he participated in many of the boyhood pursuits of the day. He enjoyed roller-skating and hockey-playing, but displayed little interest in music. When the Gershwins brought home a second-hand piano and George's older brother Ira began practicing his scales, Georges's curiosity with music was aroused and he asked to have a music teacher. (Later in their musical careers, George and Ira collaborated on several popular songs; George composed the music and Ira wrote the lyrics.) Although Ira had sparked his younger brother's interest in the piano, it was the entertaining violin-playing of George's schoolmate, Max Rosen, that truly inspired George to pursue the study of music.

When George learned that little Max Rosen would be entertaining the students at his school after recess, George thought that he would rather play outside. But as Max played, strains of beautiful violin music floated outside and George became mesmerized.

Once George decided to seriously pursue music, he studied diligently with a variety of teachers. One of the teachers who proved most helpful and inspiring to George was Charles Hambitzer. Hambitzer introduced George to the work of the famous composers Chopin, Liszt, and Debussy. Hambitzer also opened the door to the magical world of harmony and from that instructive introduction, George's musical talents soared.

When he was only sixteen, George got job with Remick's, a music publishing firm. For fifteen dollars a week, he wrote songs for singers, vaudeville performers, and producers. He was a "song-plugger" in Tin Pan Alley, the cradle of popular music in Broadway, New York. Shortly afterwards, George began working for thirty-five dollars a week at the Harms Publishing Company. Here George saw his first musical comedy, *La La Lucille*, open to a warm audience on June 12, 1919, at the Colonial Theater in Boston. Meanwhile, the comedian and singer Al Jolson adopted George's song, *Swanee*, as his own and immediately,

Swanee became a million-copy hit. George Gershwin had become famous. In the 1920s Gershwin continued his climb to fame with the musical comedies *Lady, Be Good*; *Tip-Toes*; *Oh, Kay!*; *Funny Face*; and *Girl Crazy*. His 1931 musical, *Of Thee I Sing*, was the first musical comedy, to win a Pulitzer Prize.

George Gershwin's musical talents became much sought after and he was commissioned to write many songs. Meanwhile, jazz music was becoming a popular form of American music and on November 1, 1923, George Gershwin made his debut performance as a concert pianist, at the same time helping to bring jazz to the revered art form it is today.

In 1924, Gershwin was commissioned by Paul Whiteman to write a symphony for a jazz concert Whiteman was planning. In an attempt to capture the diversity of American people—their music, speech, character, and spirit—Gershwin wrote *Rhapsody In Blue*. *Rhapsody In Blue* made musical history the night it was performed in Aeolian Hall on February 12, 1924.

Gershwin went on to write many successful scores for Broadway shows and for the Hollywood screen. Audiences embraced his fresh jazz symphonies and fell in love with such compositions as the *Concerto In F*, the *Cuban Overture*, and *An American In Paris*.

After finishing the piano score for *An American In Paris*, and writing his *Second Rhapsody*, Gershwin felt a very strong desire to write an American opera. After several experiments, Gershwin wrote *Porgy And Bess* (1935), which describes the life, suffering, and hopes of black America. The music of *Porgy And Bess* was wildly exciting and the opera included the unforgettable hits "Summertime" and "It Ain't Necessarily So." *Porgy And Bess* was the most popular opera ever written by an American.

Soon after it was discovered he had a brain tumor, Gershwin died suddenly on July 11, 1937, following an unsuccessful operation. Gershwin's great contribution of bringing the Tin Pan Alley-style of writing to "serious" music, and his use of jazz elements in symphonic music, made musical history. Gershwin's music—full of life and spirit—will live on forever.

Name_____

George Gershwin

A. I like to slurp spaghetti.

A. I like to slurp spaghetti.

B. Long and curly and springy and swirly.

A. I like to slurp spaghetti.

MATERIALS: Pencil and paper.

ACTIVITY:

1. George Gershwin used the musical format called sonata form, or the AABA method. The A, or the exposition, states the main theme or idea of the song. The second A repeats it. The B is the development which takes off from the primary theme and changes or adds new ideas. The final A, or recapitulation, goes back to "recap" the main idea. (Sometimes the recapitulation is not an exact repeat.)

1. An example of AABA is written above on this page.

3. Get a piece of paper and pencil and write lyrics to a short song using the AABA method. A good theme choice might be pets, food, the weather, or friendship.

Evaluation   Name _____

THINKING ABOUT GEORGE GERSHWIN AND ME

Respond to four or more of the following questions/statements:

1. Try to find and listen to three Gershwin recordings. List the titles of the songs and underline the one you liked best. Describe why you liked it.

2. Why do you think George Gershwin used the AABA format? Explain.

3. What theme did you use for your song and why?

4. When George Gershwin heard his schoolmate, Max Rosen, playing the violin, he became immediately inspired to study music. What schoolmate, friend, or relative has inspired you to do something you might not have thought of doing? Explain.

5. Later in life, George Gershwin wrote many songs with his older brother Ira Gershwin. Who might you collaborate with and what will you do together?

6. Write one or more paragraphs about what you have learned about this composer and/or what you have learned through your activity project relating to this composer.

George Frederick Handel
1685–1759

George Frederick Handel was born at Halle, Germany, on February 23, 1685. In the nearby town of Eisenach, a hundred miles from Halle, Johann Sebastian Bach was born one month later. Both men became famous musicians and although Bach once walked to Halle to hear Handel play, he was late and so missed Handel's performance. Thus, the two musicians never met.

George Frederick's father was a very wealthy barber-surgeon who not only cut his patrons' hair, but also performed minor operations such as pulling people's teeth and mending their broken bones. Ironically, George Frederick's father hated music so much that when church bells rang, he shut his windows; and when street musicians played their instruments, he paid them to stop. So when George Frederick was born, his sixty-two year old father even disliked the lullabies Aunt Anna sang to her baby nephew.

Aunt Anna was the sister of George Frederick's young mother and she lived in the Handel household taking care of her nephew. Even though George Handle Sr. tried to keep music away from his son (he wanted George Frederick to become a lawyer, not a musician), Aunt Anna found many ways to surround her nephew with music. When George Frederick was seven years old, she brought him a little clavichord (a small piano-like instrument) and hid it in the attic where George Handle Sr. was unlikely to hear any music. Every day George Frederick happily played the clavichord. Soon he was not only playing melodies he had heard before, but he was also making up his own music.

One day the Duke of Weissenfels, a great lover of music, sent for the famous barber-surgeon of Halle—George Frederick Sr.—as he had heard of a wonderfully successful operation where Handel had extracted a knife that a young man had accidentally swallowed. George Frederick accompanied his father on this trip and while his father attended to business in the castle, George went exploring. While exploring, George Frederick was lured by beautiful organ music to the castle's chapel, and there he met the organist who invited him to play the organ. When George Frederick played, the organist was stunned and amazed by this young child's ability. Immediately, the organist sent for the Duke who also became entranced by George Frederick's music. Both the organist and the Duke were astounded that young Handel had not received any formal music lessons. After a pause, George Handel Sr. finally consented to let his young son study music. Lessons were arranged with Friedrich Zachau, the church organist at Halle. Friedrich Zachau was a very good teacher and by the age of eleven, George Frederick was playing the harpsichord, organ, violin, and oboe. He also became the assistant organist to his teacher.

Even though young Handel was finally pursuing his heart's desire, his father still insisted that he study law. In 1702, Handel entered Halle University while still holding his position as church organist. A year later, Handel joined an orchestra in Hamburg where he composed his first operas. His very first opera, *Almira*, was written when he was twenty years old.

In 1707, Handel visited Italy where he met many famous and important people. His first Italian opera *Agrippina* (produced in Venice), quickly spread his fame throughout Italy. When he returned to Germany around 1710, Handel was appointed choir master to the Elector of Hanover. Because Handel's operas were becoming so popular and successful, he was invited to many places throughout Europe. While visiting London in 1712, Handel wrote "An Ode for the Queen's Birthday" which won him considerable acclaim and royal favor—so much so that he was given an annual salary of several hundred pounds, a great deal of money in the eighteenth century.

As luck would have it, Handel's former employer, the Elector of Hanover, became King George I of England. To honor England's new king, Handel wrote a new composition to be played during a water festival on the River Thames. King George I was so delighted with the music that Handel received a salary from the British court until he died. The famous orchestral composition is known as Handel's *Water Music*.

Handel remained in England for the rest of his life. In 1720 he was appointed the director of the Royal Academy of Music in London where he produced many operas. Because Handel followed the Italian style of opera, which was becoming unpopular in England, Handel devoted his attention to oratorios, choral works usually of a religious nature. Handel is best known for the oratorios he wrote after he was fifty-three years old. The greatest of these, *Messiah*, first performed in Dublin, Ireland, on April 13, 1742, was written in less than a month. From that day on, particularly at Christmastime, *Messiah* has been sung all over the world.

Despite his failing sight, Handel continued to write oratorios, to play the organ, and to give concerts until his death on April 14, 1759. Handel, one of the most prolific of the baroque composers and the creator of the *Messiah*, was buried in Westminster Abbey in London.

George Frederick Handel

MATERIALS: Shoe box, tape, construction paper, markers, and scissors.

ACTIVITY:

1. Handel wrote many beautiful operas. You will make an opera house for Handels's music.

2. Using the diagram above, lay the deep part of the box on its side. Next take the box top and tape it under the bottom of the shoe box flat side up.

3. Draw and color opera singers and cut them out leaving tabs of paper at the bottom. Fold and tape the tabs down so the opera singers stand up.

4. Decorate the opera house with curtains and lights made out of paper—wallpaper, crepe paper, or tissue paper.

Evaluation   Name _____

THINKING ABOUT HANDEL AND ME

Respond to four or more of the following questions/statements.

1. Handel's father believed making a lot of money was the first and foremost concern in choosing a career. Which do you think is more important: to be happy with your career or to make money? Explain.

2. Handel had a very close friend in the Hamburg Opera who was jealous of Handel's talent. Then Handel became jealous of his friend's talent. The two friends fought on stage after a performance. How do you deal with your jealousy?

3. One time, J.S. Bach walked for miles to hear Handel play, but he was late and missed the show. Have you ever made a sacrifice for something you wanted badly? Explain.

4. To please King George I, Handel played music on a barge that traveled along the Thames River. It was like a parade on water instead of on land. Describe a parade that you have seen. What kind of music did you hear? What instruments were played? What costumes were worn?

5. Write one or more paragraphs about what you have learned about this composer and/or what you have learned through your activity project relating to this composer.

Franz Joseph Haydn
(hi-duhn)
1732–1809

Franz Joseph Haydn, father of the symphony, close friend and teacher of Wolfgang Amadeus Mozart, and for a brief time, teacher of Ludwig van Beethoven; was the first of the great classical composers. The term "classical music" refers to music written between the years 1750 and 1825. Because much of the musical activity of the three great classical composers—Haydn, Mozart and Beethoven—centered around Vienna, Austria, the classical period is often called the Viennese-Classical period as well. At the beginning of the classical period, musicians were dependent on wealthy citizens and the church; musicians were considered servants to them. Gradually this changed and by 1800 composers were writing primarily for the general public.

Franz Joseph Haydn was born on March 31, 1732, in Rohrau, an Austrian village near Vienna. His father wanted him to study music, and so young Haydn was sent to live with a cousin in Vienna when he was six years old. By the time he was eight, Haydn sang soprano in the St. Stephen's Cathedral choir in Vienna. Everyone who heard him sing praised his voice. Even the Empress Marie Theresa remarked upon the beauty of Joseph's singing. For nine years, Joseph sang in the choir at St. Stephen's and when his voice began to change during his teenage years, Joseph earned his living playing in an orchestra and accompanying singers and violinists on the harpsichord. By the time Joseph was twenty-seven years old, he was well-known throughout Vienna.

After many years of hard work, Haydn was hired to be the music director and composer for the Bohemian Count Ferdinand Maximilian von Morzin. The von Morzins had their own orchestra as did many wealthy nobles of their day. It was for this family's orchestra that Haydn wrote his first symphony. Hungarian Prince Paul Esterházy, a nobleman from one of the wealthiest and most powerful families in Europe, was sitting in the audience when this symphony was performed. Prince Esterházy was charmed by Haydn's music and when the von Morzins could no longer afford to pay their musicians, Prince Esterházy asked Haydn to join his court and work for him.

So in 1761, when Haydn was twenty-nine, he joined the Esterházy service and became an assistant conductor of the orchestra. Two years later, Haydn was made conductor. As the Esterházys loved music, Haydn was kept very busy. Haydn had considerable freedom in writing music, but whenever the Estehàzys requested specific types of compositions, Haydn had to produce them. He was required to be present twice a day to receive orders and it was his duty to be in charge of all the music at the Esterházy court. During his thirty years with the Esterházy's private orchestra it became one of the finest in its time; publications of Haydn's compositions gained the family much fame throughout Europe. It was at the Esterházy estate where Haydn wrote *The Toy Symphony* for children, whom he dearly loved. While Haydn had no children of his own, he wished to write for children a symphony in which toy instruments were used. When Prince Nikolaus Esterházy died in 1790, Haydn was dismissed by Esterházy's son. In gratitude of his thirty years of service, Haydn was given a lifelong pension.

After leaving the Esterhàzy's home, Haydn visited London and gave a series of concerts. There he also wrote the *London Symphonies*—his last twelve symphonies—which include the famous *Surprise Symphony*. Because the English people were so honored and enthusiastic to have Haydn working in London, Oxford University conferred on him an Honorary Doctorate of Music.

Haydn composed more than one hundred symphonies. Although he did not write the very first symphony, he is called "the father of the symphony" because he developed the symphonic form to perfection, carefully defining and arranging it. The combination of instruments Haydn used in his symphonies became the basis of today's symphony orchestra. In addition to his works for a full orchestra Haydn also wrote over eighty string quartets (compositions for two violins, a viola, and a cello). Some of Haydn's popular quartets include *The Bird*, *The Sun Quartets,* and *The Emperor*. He also composed numerous concertos, sonatas, operas, and oratorios. Two of his most famous oratorios are *The Creation* and *The Seasons*.

On March 27, 1808, a great concert was held to celebrate Haydn's seventy-sixth birthday. It was little more than a year after this honorary event that the Austrian composer of "The Emperor's Hymn," Austria's national anthem, died in his sleep May 31, 1809.

Name _____

Franz Joseph Haydn

MATERIALS: Paper for a two-dimensional clock or throw-aways for a three-dimensional clock, crayons or markers, scissors.

ACTIVITY:

1. Have you ever heard a musical clock? Haydn wrote music for a musical clock.

2. Design a clock that you have never seen before. Then create a tune and/or words that you would like your clock to play at a specific time.

3. Share information about your clock with others. For example, you might hum the tune of the music you wrote for your clock when you put the clock hands on a specific hour.

Evaluation   Name _____

THINKING ABOUT HAYDN AND ME

Respond to four or more of the following questions/statements:

1. Haydn often worked independently, especially when he was living with his cousins. What is an independent worker?

2. Haydn is often called the "Father of Symphony." Why was he given this title?

3. Research and describe the clothing that Haydn wore as a child and as an adult. How was his clothing different from the clothing that we wear today? How was it the same?

4. Write the names of at least five of Haydn's symphonies. Put a star by the ones you have heard.

5. How would you feel about playing an instrument for a king, queen, or president? Write how you would feel about receiving the invitation to play for this person.

6. Write one or more paragraphs about what you have learned about this composer and/or what you have learned through your activity project relating to this composer.

Fanny Mendelssohn
(mehn-dl-sun)
1805–1847

Fanny Mendelssohn is most commonly remembered as the beloved older sister of Felix Mendelssohn, a German romantic composer who was the creator of the famous oratorios *St. Paul* and *Elijah*. Had Fanny been born a hundred years later, when the work of women was beginning to be as honored and respected as its male counterparts', she would have been known as a famous composer in her own right.

The oldest child in a very prominent German-Jewish family, Fanny Mendelssohn was born in Hamburg, Germany, in 1805. When she and her brother Felix were very young, their mother Leah began to give them music lessons. Fanny's talent was apparent—her mother told her friends that little Fanny had "Bach-fugue" fingers. The renowned eighteenth century German baroque composer, Johann Sebastian Bach, was the master of the fugue, a musical composition in which the first melody is continually repeated and imitated throughout the entire piece. By the time she was thirteen years old, Fanny could play Bach's entire *Well-Tempered Clavier* by memory. (*The Well-Tempered Clavier*, known today as *The Well-Tempered Clavichord*, is divided into two parts with each part consisting of twenty-four preludes and twenty-four fugues, one in each of the major and minor keys—it was a great accomplishment that young Fanny knew the entire piece by heart.)

At the same time Felix, who was four years younger than Fanny, began to surpass his sister in musical accomplishments. When Felix was nine years old he started performing publicly. Many famous people, among them the composer Carl Maria von Weber and the great poet Goethe, delighted in his music. When Felix's teacher took him to visit Goethe, Fanny asked that Felix remember every word Goethe said so that he could recount his incredible experience with her. The exchange of letters between Felix and Fanny is a record of on-going observations and insights shared by these siblings.

Despite Felix's shining accomplishments—he was an admired composer by the time he was twenty—Fanny continued to pursue her own musical career. Felix and Fanny were always close to one another and Fanny adored her younger brother. Although Fanny too had become a popular pianist and composed songs, cantatas, oratorios, and operas, she spent more time promoting Felix's work and neglecting her own. Fanny even let Felix publish six of her own songs under his name. Many of Fanny's own compositions remain unpublished in the manuscript collections of The New York Public Library and the Library of Congress.

Later in life, Fanny married an artist, Wilhelm Hensel, who often had drawn pictures of the Mendelssohn family; Felix married a French woman, Cécile Jeanrenaud.

Until their death, Fanny and Felix remained close to one another. While rehearsing Felix's *Walpurgisnacht* in the family auditorium, Fanny suddenly collapsed and died. Upon hearing of his sister's death, Felix became seriously ill. The tragic news of Fanny's death was more than Felix could bear. He never recovered from the shock. Felix died six months after his beloved sister Fanny.

Name _____

Fanny Mendelssohn

MATERIALS: Writing paper and pencil.

ACTIVITY:

1. You are a journalist and Fanny Mendelssohn has arrived in your city.

2. Write about her arrival, concert, and departure for your local newspaper.

3. As a journalist you will want to be objective, truthful, and respectful.

Name _____

THINKING ABOUT FANNY MENDELSSOHN AND ME

Respond to four or more of the following questions/statements:

1. Describe the reactions to Fanny Mendelssohn's musical compositions when she was alive. If she were living today, how do you think her work would be treated?

2. Why do you think Fanny let Felix publish some of her compositions under his name rather than her own name?

3. Research music books to find works of three female composers. List the names of these women and their compositions.

4. Fanny Mendelssohn was born in 1805 and died in 1847. How old was she when she died? Shortly after Fanny's death her brother Felix died. Felix was born in 1809 and died in 1847. How old was he when he died?

5. As a brother and sister, Felix and Fanny shared a special friendship. Do you have a brother or a sister who is also a special friend? If so, what do you do for each other?

6. Write one or more paragraphs about what you have learned about this composer and/or what you have learned through your activity project relating to this composer.

Felix Mendelssohn
(mehn-dl-sun)
1809–1847

Like the famous classical composers Mozart and Beethoven, Felix Mendelssohn's musical talent was evident at an early age. But unlike many other famous composers, he bore none of the financial struggles common among them.

Felix Mendelssohn was born in Hamburg, Germany on February 3, 1809, the son of a wealthy and cultured banker. Although Felix was one of four children, he was particularly fond of his older sister, Fanny. Fanny and Felix adored each other and remained very close throughout their lifetimes.

When Felix was four years old his mother began teaching piano to Fanny and him. The children made rapid progress and while their mother remarked on Fanny's "Bach-fugue fingers," little did she know that it would be her son, Felix, who would rediscover Bach's genius and present his music to the world.

When the Mendelssohn family moved to Berlin, Felix began to study composition with the famous music teacher, Carl Zelter. By the time Felix was ten years old, he was performing publicly and by the time he was twelve, he was composing seriously. Felix's first known work was a cantata, which is a vocal work for chorus, soloist, and orchestra that is performed without staging. Carl Zelter was impressed with his pupil's talent and so he took young Felix on a trip to Weimar to visit the great poet, Goethe. Goethe was so affected by Felix's playing, he invited Felix and Zelter to be his guests for two weeks. Every day Felix played the piano and improvised for Goethe who delighted in his performing. Felix carefully observed the seventy-two-year-old Goethe so that he might capture the memorable things Goethe did and said in his letters to his sister Fanny. In later years, Felix became almost as famous for his letter-writing as he did for his music.

When Felix was only seventeen, he wrote an overture to Shakespeare's *A Midsummer Night's Dream*. This musical work was considered by many to be the most beautiful music ever written by someone so young. Several years after this, Felix, always a passionate student of Bach's (who had died almost eighty years earlier), reintroduced Bach's *Passion According to St. Matthew* with great success.

Soon after this, Felix made one of many subsequent trips to England. While visiting England, he also visited Scotland and the Hebrides nearby where he saw Fingal's cave, a formation of two tall rocks making an arch over the sea below. Inspired by this vivid landscape and natural beauty, Felix composed an overture entitled the *Hebrides*, or *Fingal's Cave* overture. In this music, one can hear all the lonely echoes and sounds which Felix heard on that visit. Felix Mendelssohn was one of the first to write independent concert overtures. Usually, overtures functioned as musical introductions to operas or oratorios; the concert-overture, however, is complete in itself.

While in England, Felix published his first book of piano pieces, *Songs Without Words*. One especially lovely piece from this book is entitled *Spring Song*. Felix then settled in the city of Düsseldorf, Germany, where he became general musical director. In 1835, Felix became conductor of the famous Gewandhaus Orchestra and in 1843, he founded the Leipzig Conservatory, one of the most famous music schools in the world.

Felix married Cécile Jeanrenaud, a beautiful daughter of a French minister, and they eventually became the parents of five children. Despite these happy and successful years, there were two incidents which greatly saddened Felix, one of which was the death of his father. In memory of Abraham Mendelssohn, Felix composed *St. Paul*, and *Elijah*, which remain two of the most famous oratorios in musical history.

On returning from a trip to England in 1847, Felix was doubly saddened to learn of the death of his sister, Fanny. It was said that Felix lost consciousness when he heard of her death and afterwards never regained his full health. Felix died six months later in Leipzig, on November 4, 1847. He was buried in Berlin and greatly mourned by all who knew him or his music. But Felix Mendelssohn's beautiful music lives on today, enchanting listeners with melodic symphonies, overtures, piano compositions, and oratorios.

Felix Mendelssohn

MATERIALS: White drawing paper, crayons or markers, pencil, and Mendelssohn recordings.

ACTIVITY:

1. Felix Mendelssohn was a very talented and successful musician. He often looked at nature's colors and movement to get ideas for his music. He also closely observed the people and culture of each country he visited.

2. Listen to some Felix Mendelssohn recordings. Check the titles and descriptions to see if the any pieces pertain to an area of land or a special place. Try to find one that does.

3. Listen to the selected music before you start to draw. Then draw a picture that describes the nature scenes, colors, and people you "see" in Mendelssohn's music.

4. When you are ready, pencil in your idea and then begin to add color. While you are creating your drawing, play the Mendelssohn composition again.

Evaluation   Name _____

THINKING ABOUT FELIX MENDELSSOHN AND ME

Respond to four or more of the following questions/statements.

1. What musical piece did you listen to and what does your drawing look like? Be descriptive.

2. Who was Felix close to as a child and an adult? Do you have a brother or sister or cousin that you feel very close to? Explain your answer.

3. When Felix Mendelssohn was a child, he had the honor of meeting a person who was very famous. Have you ever met someone famous? If not, who would you like to meet? Why?

4. If you have studied any other composer in this book so far (especially Schubert), try to answer this question: Do you think Felix Mendelssohn had an easier life as a musician/composer than those you have studied so far? How did Mendelssohn's life as musician/composer differ from Schubert's? Be as specific as you can.

5. How does Mendelssohn's music affect you? Draw a picture of what you are imagining while you listen to Mendelssohn's music. Be as descriptive as you can.

6. Write one or more paragraphs about what you have learned about this composer and/or what you have learned through your activity project relating to this composer.

Wolfgang Amadeus Mozart
(moht-sart)
1756–1791

Wolfgang Amadeus Mozart was a three-year-old boy when he began to imitate the musical compositions his eight-year-old sister, Maria Anna (nicknamed Nannerl), played on the harpsichord. When Wolfgang's father, Leopold, heard his young son playing the harpsichord, he was astounded by the boy's memory and musicality.

As a court violinist and concertmaster in the employ of the Archbishop of Salzburg, Leopold Mozart was a talented musician himself. Leopold was also an ambitious father and he taught Wolfgang and Nannerl the basic elements of music at a very early age. With Wolfgang, periods of musical instruction started very early—when Wolfgang was four years old, his father began his formal training in music, and by the age of five Wolfgang was composing his own pieces. At this same age Wolfgang was also teaching himself to play the violin.

Leopold Mozart was immensely proud of his children's musical accomplishments. He decided to leave their home in Salzburg, Austria, and take Nannerl and Wolfgang on a concert tour. So in 1762, Leopold took his children to Munich, Bavaria (now Germany), where they performed for the Elector Maximilian Joseph of Bavaria. Shortly after the trip to Bavaria the entire Mozart family, including Wolfgang and Nannerl's mother, set off for Vienna where the children played the clavier for the Emperor Francis I and the Empress Maria Theresa at the palace of Schönbrunn. The Mozart children soon became know as the "Wonder Children." Wolfgang's performances were especially remarkable—not only did his musical ability captivate all who heard him, but his joyous and unspoiled spirit affected all those around him. Wolfgang and Nannerl played for the King and Queen at the Versailles Palace outside of Paris before going onto London where they played for the King and Queen of England. There Wolfgang played King George III's organ and accompanied Queen Charlotte in song. While visiting England, eight-year-old Wolfgang composed several sonatas for violin and harpsichord, and a number of symphonies.

Later, Wolfgang toured Italy and continued to amaze the audiences there. While in Rome, Wolfgang had the opportunity to hear the Sistine Chapel choir sing *Miserere* during Holy Week. Young Mozart loved the beautiful music so much that when he returned home, he wrote the entire work on paper from memory.

When Wolfgang returned to Salzburg, he was appointed to serve as concert-master and work with his father under the Archbishop of Salzburg. Both Wolfgang and Leopold worked exclusively for the Archbishop, writing and composing new pieces of music especially for him. Mozart found this work dull and much preferred to write music from his own inspirations. Much against his father's will, young Mozart contrived to have himself dismissed from the Archbishop's employ in 1781.

Mozart then went to Vienna where he met Constanze Weber, the daughter of his landlord, and they married in 1782. Mozart's musical productivity was very impressive, but he was often not paid sufficiently for his work. Mozart and Constanze spent most of their married life in poverty. During this time Mozart wrote three of his great operas: *Don Giovanni*, *The Magic Flute*, and *The Marriage of Figaro*. Audiences were enthusiastic about his operas but Mozart made little money from any of these popular works. He had to borrow money from his friends in order to support his family—his wife Constanze and their two children—but he never had enough money to repay his debts.

While Mozart was finishing *The Magic Flute* in 1791, he received a mysterious private commission to compose a Requiem Mass, music for someone who had died. The mysterious stranger who requested the Requiem promised to pay well for it. Mozart never finished the piece, though now the *Requiem* is one of his most famous works. Mozart died on December 5, 1791, while trying to finish composing the work as his friends rehearsed the score in his room.

In 1991, to commemorate the two hundredth anniversary of Mozart's death, cities around the world—from Salzburg, the place of Mozart's birth, to New York at Lincoln Center where Mozart's 373 orchestral works, 227 songs, 98 sacred and dramatic pieces, and much else is performed—honored and celebrated this most gifted and expressive of classical composers. While Mozart was only thirty-five years old when he died in Vienna, the music he created remains timeless.

Activity Sheet   Name _____

Wolfgang Amadeus Mozart

MATERIALS: Paper, pencil, a recording of Mozart's music.

ACTIVITY:

1. Mozart was a clever child. He used to make up funny songs using strange words that would sometimes rhyme.

2. Like Mozart, you will compose a funny song. Be original with your words. Make them up so they rhyme with each other. Your song can be based on an imaginary place, person, or thing.

3. Try to sing your song with one of Mozart's musical works.

Name _____

THINKING ABOUT MOZART AND ME

Respond to four or more of the following questions/stastements:

1. Is your childhood in any way similar to Mozart's childhood? How is it different?

2. What inspired you to write the funny verses you wrote in the activity?

3. You have the chance to travel to far away lands and perform for kings and queens who give you gifts and admiration. What would you do in your performance? (Think about the things you do best.)

4. By the age of six, Mozart had already played for several kings and queens and had become famous. How might your personality change if you were to become famous?

5. Mozart was not a wealthy man even though he was a popular composer. Pretend you are Mozart's financial manager. What advice would you give him?

6. Write one or more paragraphs about what you have learned about this composer and/or what you have learned through your activity project relating to this composer.

Cole Porter
1891–1964

A chronicler of high society, Cole Porter captured the sophisticated, urbane glamour of the thirties and forties in his lyrics and music. He always knowingly portrayed high society with a wink and a nudge. Cole Porter, tunesmith extraordinaire, was unmatched for his witty, sophisticated lyrics and lively energy. Among his many popular and successful musicals are *Anything Goes*; *Kiss Me, Kate*; *Can-Can*; and *Silk Stockings*.

Cole Porter was born in Peru, Indiana, on June 1, 1891. He was the third child of Kate Cole Porter and Samuel Fenwick Porter, but he was the only baby to survive infancy. His mother encouraged his love for music and insisted he practice his violin and piano every day. Cole's father instilled in his son a love for words and frequently read poetry to him. Cole Porter was born into a wealthy family and until his death, he lived in luxury. His grandfather, a lumber and coal tycoon, feared his grandson would live in poverty if he sought music as a profession and urged young Cole to give up his pursuit of music. Fortunately, young Cole did not heed his grandfather's warnings.

Porter had a song published when he was eleven years old and continued to publish songs while he was a student at Yale and Harvard, prestigious universities on the East Coast. While at Harvard Law School, Porter decided to drop out in order to study music seriously. Porter was an extremely dedicated and hard-working songwriter, but even in his hardest years he lived in elegance as a result of his family's vast fortune and his marriage to the wealthy Linda Lee Thomas.

In 1920 and 1921, Porter studied music in Paris. He drew much inspiration from this romantic city and his first Broadway success was entitled *Paris* (1928). This success was followed by *Fifty Million Frenchmen*, *Gay Divorce*, and *Anything Goes*. Many of the themes in his musicals were based on the lives of the very wealthy upper-class with whom Porter socialized.

Cole Porter wrote music every day; between the ages of ten and sixty-six he wrote over eight hundred songs. Porter's most productive decade was the 1930s when his humorous, bouncy lyrics made life more bearable during the hard times of the Depression. But in 1937, near the end of his productive songwriting decade, Porter's legs were severely crushed in a horseback riding accident in Long Island. He was confined to a wheelchair and twenty-one years after the accident his right leg had to be amputated. Despite his lifelong confinement to a wheelchair and endurance of constant pain, Porter continued to write music until the amputation in 1958. His popular and successful musicals include: *Du Barry Was a Lady* (1939), *Panama Hattie* (1940), *Mexican Hayride* (1944), *Kiss Me, Kate* (1948), *Can-Can* (1953), and *Silk Stockings* (1955). He also wrote music for eight movies including *Born to Dance* (1936), *Rosalie* (1937), and *High Society* (1956), and for a 1958 television production of *Aladdin*.

Cole Porter's songs—imaginative, witty, and sophisticated—mirror the life he enjoyed. Among his most famous songs: "Begin the Beguine," "Night and Day," "I've Got You Under My Skin," and "You're the Top," we can hear his unmistakable style and the genius of his musical abilities. For many admiring listeners, Cole Porter's music will always remain "the top."

Name _____

Cole Porter

MATERIALS: Paper, pencil, a recording of Cole Porter's music.

ACTIVITY:

1. Cole Porter was a very talented songwriter. His music is still popular today.

2. You are a music critic. You will write a critique on one of Cole Porter's songs. Listen carefully to the lyrics. What is the song saying to you? What feelings does the music evoke?

3. Think about what the music would mean to your parents, family members, or friends.

4. Below, write a brief description of the song and tell what you think of it and why.

_____

_____

_____

_____

_____

_____

_____

_____

_____

_____

_____

_____

_____

_____

_____

_____

Name _____

THINKING ABOUT COLE PORTER AND ME

Respond to four or more of the following questions/statements:

1. Pretend you are Cole Porter. Read a classmate's critique of your work (from page 61). What does it say about your music? How do you feel about it? Explain.

2. If you were a songwriter, would you give up your career if the critics and public did not like your work? Explain.

3. If Cole Porter were alive today, do you think he would be surprised that his songs are still popular? Explain.

4. Why do you think songs, types of cars, hairstyles, and some styles of clothing stay popular after so many years?

5. Cole Porter is considered an American standard. Make a list of people, places, and things that you consider an American standard. For example, hamburgers, pizza, baseball, the Grand Canyon, and New York City may be considered American standards.

6. Write one or more paragraphs about what you have learned about this composer and/or what you have learned through your activity project relating to this composer.

Sergei Sergeivitch Prokofiev (pro-koff-yeff) 1891–1953

Sergei Sergeivitch Prokofiev was born in Soutzovka, Russia, on April 23, 1891 to a music-loving mother and a father. By the time he was six years old, Sergei was improvising on the piano and writing his own musical compositions. When young Sergei was nine years old, he wrote an opera entitled *The Giant* which was performed at his uncle's estate. At eleven years of age, Sergei began to study music seriously. Sergei Sergeivitch Prokofiev not only became a brilliant pianist, he also became the leading Soviet composer of his time. Although he became prolific in all areas of composition—operas, ballets, sonatas, concertos, symphonies, and music for motion pictures—Prokofiev is best known for his symphonic fairy tale for children, *Peter and the Wolf*.

Prokofiev's first teacher, Reinhold Glière, recognized the energetic and creative spirit in his eleven-year-old student, so did not overburden the young musician with a rigorous course of study. Glière allowed for enough freedom in Prokofiev's studies to nurture his budding creativity.

From 1904 to 1914, Prokofiev attended the St. Petersburg Conservatory and studied piano, composition, and conducting. At the St. Petersburg commencement exercises on May 24, 1914, Prokofiev played a piano concerto he had written in 1911 as his graduation piece. He won first prize: a grand piano.

In 1914, when Prokofiev was twenty-three years old, he composed his first major orchestral work, *Scythian Suite*. It was first performed under Prokofiev in January 1916 and was regarded as a first-cousin to Russian composer Igor Stravinsky's masterpiece, *Rite of Spring*.

Prokofiev left Russian in 1918 and lived in Germany and Paris for the next sixteen years. Throughout his musical career he was inspired by great artistic forerunners including the composers Wolfgang Amadeus Mozart and Modest Mussorgsky; the novelist Fyodor Dostoyevsky; and the choreographer and founder of the famous Ballet Russes, Sergei Diaghilev.

Prokofiev also made many guest appearances in the United States as pianist in various performances of his work. On December 30, 1921, the Chicago Opera Company presented the first Prokofiev opera production, *Love for the Three Oranges*, one of Prokofiev's most celebrated works.

In 1934, Prokofiev went home to Russia and settled in Moscow. Here Prokofiev composed many great works which are often identified with the Soviet Union. In 1936, Prokofiev wrote the *Russian Overture*, and in the following year he wrote a cantata (a vocal work for chorus, soloist, and orchestra that is performed without staging) based on the writings and speeches of Marx, Lenin, and Stalin. This cantata was written to commemorate the twentieth anniversary of the Soviet Revolution. Among Prokofiev's other successful works are the operas *Simeon Kotko* (1940) and *War and Peace* (1942), the ballets *Romeo and Juliet* (1936) and *The Stone Flower* (1954), the cantata *Alexander Nevsky* (1939), and *Symphony No. 5* (1945), considered the best of his seven symphonies. But despite all of these major works, it was a fairy tale set to music, written in a sudden surge of inspiration, that brought fame to Prokofiev. The musical tale for children was the masterpiece, *Peter and the Wolf*.

Peter and the Wolf is a musical story in which different instruments of the orchestra represent different characters. The story tells of a young boy who disobeys his grandfather in an attempt to save the lives of his friends—the bird, the duck, and the cat—from a hungry wolf. The character of Peter is represented by the string quartet, the bird by the flute, the duck by the oboe, the cat by the clarinet, the grandfather by the bassoon, the wolf by the horns, and the shout of the hunters by the kettle drums and bass drums. Prokofiev was so inspired to write and compose the music for the story, that he is credited for finishing the whole piano score in four days—the full score was completed a week later. *Peter and the Wolf* was first performed at the Children's Theater in Moscow on May 2, 1936. Since its premiere, this musical story has appeared in concerts and ballets, in books, and on records all over the world. Because it communicates to children and adults of all ages, *Peter and the Wolf* is a masterpiece—Sergei Sergeivitch Prokofiev its masterful creator.

Name _____

Sergei Sergeivitch Prokofiev

MATERIALS: Paper, pencil, and real or rhythm band instruments. (If instruments are not available, participants can use their voices to make sounds to represent specific instruments.)

ACTIVITY:

1. Listen to a tape or record of *Peter and the Wolf*.

2. Write a play using instruments to represent specific characters such as animals, toys, or other objects.

3. Share your play with others.

4. On the back of this page, write a summary of your play.

Evaluation   Name _____

THINKING ABOUT SERGEI PROKOFIEV AND ME

Respond to four or more of the following questions/statements:

1. Sergei Prokofiev was a creative person from childhood through adulthood. What creative things do you do?

2. List at least five instruments. Then write what animals, objects, or actions they could each represent.

3. Prokofiev made many guest appearances. If you were to give a guest appearance, where would you like to perform and what would you do for your performance?

4. Be creative! Write a different beginning and/or ending to *Peter and the Wolf*.

5. What did you like most about writing/presenting your own play?

6. Write one or more paragraphs about what you have learned about this composer and/or what you have learned through your activity project relating to this composer.

Franz Schubert
(shoo-bert)
1797–1828

For many years the city of Vienna, Austria, was the center for many important musical events. Composers such as Haydn, Mozart, and Beethoven all at one time or another performed in Vienna. One composer, however, Franz Peter Schubert, was actually born in Vienna on January 31, 1797. At the time of Schubert's birth, Beethoven was already recognized as a fine pianist. The great composer Mozart had died only six years earlier; and Haydn, who was the teacher of both Mozart and Beethoven, had recently written "The Emperor's Hymn" which became the Austrian national anthem.

Franz Schubert was born into a large and humble family. His father was a schoolmaster who encouraged an appreciation for fine music in his household. Frequently, the Schubert family would gather in the evenings and listen to one another play and perform chamber music. Young Franz received his first musical instruction from his father, an amateur violinist. Franz's older brother guided him at the piano, but Franz had already mastered many elements of music by himself. Franz's father arranged for the parish choirmaster, Herr Michael Holzer, to be Franz's musical instructor. Franz quickly became Herr Holzer's prized pupil.

Franz also loved to sing. By the time he was eleven years old he was performing as a soloist in Vienna and nearby suburbs. He was quickly admitted to the Imperial Church Choir in Vienna which offered the best musical education for young boys. When Franz and his father arrived at the Imperial Choir School for Franz's audition, many of the other boys present teased and ridiculed Franz because of his shabby, dusty clothes and big eyeglasses. Much to Franz's delight, however, he was one of only two boys admitted into the school.

At the Imperial Choir school, Franz was appointed first violinist in the orchestra which he was occasionally allowed to conduct. Franz studied music theory and began composing many melodies, songs, and quartets. He spent all his allowance on manuscript paper, writing one beautiful composition after another. One of his favorite pieces was *Moments Musicaux in F Minor*.

In 1813, Franz was sixteen years old when he wrote his first symphony; the following year he completed his first Mass. Music was clearly Franz's passion and destiny. But Franz's father wished for him to be an elementary teacher in his school. Finally persuaded, Franz taught for three years, even though he did not enjoy his work. Outside of his school duties, he continued to write hundreds of songs. One of his most beautiful and dramatic works, inspired by the German poet Goethe, was written at this time. It was the art song entitled "Erl King."

Franz's father eventually realized how unhappy Franz was teaching at the school in the Viennese suburbs. He finally accepted, though quite angrily, Franz's resignation. In 1816, Franz left the school to pursue composing music in Vienna. There Schubert wrote with incredible flourish and speed, he never made much money from selling his compositions, giving music lessons, or occasionally performing. Schubert did have, however, a faithful following of close friends who believed in his genius and who consistently supported him, both emotionally and financially. This group of friends—fellow musicians, poets, and artists—called themselves the "Schubertians" in honor of their friend, Franz Schubert.

Living in Vienna at the same time as Schubert was the composer Ludwig van Beethoven, who was gathering fame as one of the greatest of all instrumental composers. Many times on the streets of Vienna, Schubert would pass Beethoven, whom he greatly admired. But Schubert was shy and he never introduced himself to the man he greatly looked up to. When Beethoven died in 1827, Schubert had the honor of serving as a pall bearer at Beethoven's funeral. Schubert's health began to wane and a year after Beethoven's death, on November 19, 1828, at the age of thirty-one, Schubert died as well. He is buried next to Beethoven where today in Vienna thousands of admirers decorate both graves with flowers.

Schubert's music was never fully appreciated during his lifetime. But today, this great romantic composer is best know for his over six hundred *lieder*, (German art songs). An art song was typically set to a poem and often performed during a recital. It subtly mixed interdependent vocal and piano parts. Few composers have ever matched Schubert's gift for melody, and among his most famous songs which express emotion through both words and music are "Serenade" and "Ave Maria."

In addition to his art songs, Schubert composed eight symphonies. His most famous one—*Unfinished Symphony*—has only two movements instead of the usual four movements. Schubert never heard his symphony performed during his lifetime, nor did he hear his great masterpiece, *Symphony in C Major*, which was written the year he died.

At the time of his death, Schubert's manuscripts drew hardly any money at the auction held after his burial. Now, however, the manuscripts bearing the pure, charming melodies of Franz Schubert are priceless museum pieces.

Activity Sheet   Name _____

Franz Schubert

Example:

J oyful

e nthusiasic

h **a** ppy

n eat

fu **n** ny

n **i** ce

pl **e** asant

MATERIALS: 9" x 12" sheet of colored construction paper, crayons or markers, pencil.

ACTIVITY:

1. Using the example given above, write Schubert's full name and find adjectives to describe him as a musician an composer.

2. You may use letters in Schubert's name for any part of the words you choose, the letters of his name do not necessarily need to be the first letter of a word.

3. Write in pencil first and leave space between each letter of his name so you can comfortably fit in the adjectives.

Evaluation   Name_____

THINKING ABOUT SCHUBERT AND ME

Respond to four or more of the following questions/statements:

1. List the adjectives you used to describe Schubert. Explain why you picked these words.

2. Schubert first learned to play music when he got the chance to practice in a piano repair shop. Did you ever get a chance to do something that was very beneficial? Explain.

3. Did you ever compete in an event or a contest for a special honor? Explain your competition and then explain Schubert's.

4. What very hard decision did Schubert have to make? Did you ever have a conflict where you were forced to make a difficult decision? Explain.

5. Who were the Schubertians? Do you belong to any special groups or organizations? Explain.

6. Write one or more paragraphs about what you have learned about this composer and/or what you have learned through your activity project relating to this composer.

Clara Wieck Schumann
(shoo-mahn)
1819–1896

The famed romantic composer Frédéric François Chopin declared Clara Schumann the only pianist capable of doing justice to his work. The daughter of one of Germany's most noted piano teachers, Clara Josephine Wieck was born on September 13, 1819, in Leipzig, Germany. Her father, Friedrich Wieck, had among his many pupils the renowned romantic composer, Robert Schumann. Clara's musical talents were apparent at an early age and by nine years old, she was the best advertisement for her father's teaching ability. Friedrich Wieck's little girl was known throughout Germany for her wonderful piano playing. When Robert Schumann arrived at the Wieck home to begin his piano studies there, Clara was only eleven years old. His fondness for young people clearly evident, Clara and her brothers loved playing games with Robert Schumann. Not surprisingly, Robert Schumann wrote some of the best piano music available for children learning to play the piano. Schumann's *Kinderscenen* (*Scenes from Childhood*) was published in 1838, and his *Album for the Young*, was published in 1848. Little did young Clara know how much she was to inspire the future compositions of this German composer.

By the time she was sixteen, Clara was one of the best pianists of her generation—and she and Robert Schumann had fallen in love. Clara's father was strongly against their courtship and frequently took Clara on long European tours to separate her from Robert. Herr Wieck felt Clara was too young and Schumann's future was too uncertain for the two of them to be in love. But despite these objections, Clara and Robert Schumann were married in 1840, shortly before Clara turned twenty-one.

Robert Schumann's productivity flourished during this happy time. The year he and Clara were married he composed over one hundred German *lieder* (art songs). Clara was also a composer and Robert used many passages from her work in his own compositions. In the mid-nineteenth century it was difficult and highly unusual for a woman, even as talented and accomplished as Clara, to write and publish her own music. When she and Robert were married, it became inconvenient for her to work every day at the piano since Robert was often composing or practicing at the piano himself. Clara wanted to continue performing and touring, but Robert found it difficult to work while he was touring with her.

On one occasion, Robert accompanied Clara to the court of a German prince where she was to play. The German prince had not heard of Robert Schumann and wondered what instrument he played. Robert was uncomfortable being overshadowed by his beautiful and talented wife and his jealousy may well have made him reluctant to tour with Clara.

While today we may see the unfairness between the working situations of Robert and Clara, women during Clara's time did not often have careers outside of the home. So Clara frequently worried about what was to become of her work. As she and Robert had more children—they eventually had eight—Clara found less time to devote to her own musicianship. Despite the rigors of family life, Clara learned hundreds of piano works and became the first pianist to play entire concerts by memory.

Clara played her husband's music and championed it wherever she went. Undoubtedly, Clara's influence and contribution to her husband's work is immeasurable and we can only speculate about the great professional sacrifices she made in order that her husband's work be more secure.

In 1853, the Schumanns befriended the German romantic composer Johannes Brahms. Brahms became a devoted friend, financially helping Clara when she was pregnant with her eighth child and her husband Robert was in an asylum. Brahms became an ardent and loyal admirer of Clara Schumann. His last work, *Four Serious Songs*, was written in anticipation of Clara's death but he would not actually hear it performed because he was too overcome with emotion.

Brahms and Clara Schumann promoted performances of her husband's works after he died in 1856. In later years, from 1872 to 1892, Clara headed the piano department at the Frankfurt Conservatory. She died on May 20, 1896, in Frankfurt. Brahms became very ill immediately after her death and he died less than a year later.

Clara Schumann

MATERIALS: Pencil, paper or tagboard, crayons or markers.

ACTIVITY:

1. Read about Clara Schumann. Think about the clothes that were in style, how people traveled from one place to another, and what buildings looked like during the times she lived.

2. Brainstorm various plans for posters that will advertise one of Clara Schumann's concerts. Then design a poster from your favorite plan.

3. Share your poster with others. You might tell how you got your idea for the poster and what you thought about as you designed it.

Name _____

THINKING ABOUT CLARA SCHUMANN AND ME

Respond to four or more of the following questions/statements:

1. Clara Schumann could play entire concerts by memory. Learn the lyrics to a song or a poem that you have never heard before. Then write the lyrics or poem by memory.

2. Why was it more difficult for Clara to get her music published than it was for her husband, Robert Schumann?

3. Clara often let Robert use passages from her work in his compositions. Have you ever helped someone achieve something?

4. Johannes Brahms was a loyal friend of Clara's and admired her greatly. Do you have a friend or relative like Brahms? Explain.

5. Clara used her musical ability to entertain a German prince. List ten or more ways we use music in our world.

6. Write one or more paragraphs about what you have learned bout this composer and/or what you have learned through your activity project relating to this composer.

Robert Schumann
(shoo-mahn)
1810–1856

Robert Schumann was the leader of the romantic school of composers. The romantic composers placed great importance on personal feelings and emotions. When they felt sad, they wrote somber music, and when they felt happy, they wrote lively music. The romantic period of music (1825–1900) was exciting and revolutionary. Some of the great romantic composers include Felix Mendelssohn, Frédéric Chopin, Franz Liszt, and Johannes Brahms.

Robert Schumann was born in Zwickau, Germany, on June 8, 1810. His father, a bookseller and publisher, encouraged Robert's musical talent. Robert began piano lessons at the age of eight and soon afterwards was composing small dances. When Robert was still young his father died, and because the study of law seemed more respectable than music, Robert's mother encourage him to go to law school. So in 1828, Robert entered the University of Leipzig; however, he devoted more of his time to music and writing than studying law. Finally, after consulting with Friedrich Wieck, the greatest piano teacher in Germany, Robert's mother agreed to let Robert pursue his musical studies full-time.

Robert worked hard under Friedrich Wieck; he practiced long hours and made splendid progress. Wieck had a talented eleven-year-old daughter, Clara, who was known all over Germany for her incredible piano playing. One day when Wieck was away on tour with Clara, Robert injured the fourth finger on his right hand. Unfortunately, the injury forced Robert to abandon all his hopes as a career pianist and he realized he would have to succeed on his strengths as a composer and as a writer, promoting the music of his generation. It was at this time that Robert and a group of friends began a music journal in Leipzig.

Although Schumann is best remembered for his great compositions, he is also credited for important writings on music. In 1833, Schumann helped found the *New Journal for Music*. In addition to editing the journal for nine years, Schumann also wrote many articles for it until 1853. Several of these articles helped establish the early reputation of such composers as Johannes Brahms of Germany and Frédéric Chopin of Poland. Schumann recognized and praised the work of his talented contemporaries and always kept his eyes and ears open for new, emerging talent. Schumann was thus known as a great critic who enjoyed much success at explaining the works of other composers to the public.

About the time he started the *New Journal for Music*, Robert realized he was in love with Clara Wieck, the daughter of his piano teacher. Friedrich Wieck was very unhappy when he learned that Robert and Clara were in love. Wieck thought his daughter, now sixteen years old, was too young. Wieck also knew that Clara was one of the best pianists of her generation and he did not want a marriage to end his daughter's musical career before it had even begun. Robert wrote some of his most exquisite piano compositions for Clara; his many sonatas written at this time were actually love poems to Clara set to music. Clara's father forbade them to see one another and for several months they were separated. Unhappy and alone, Robert's only consolation was his music. In his piano composition, *Sonata in F Minor*, his unhappiness and loneliness are evident. Finally in 1840, despite Wieck's objections, Clara and Robert were married.

During their first year of marriage, Schumann wrote over one hundred songs, many inspired by Clara, with whom he was much in love. These German *lieder* (art songs) were the most beautiful that any composer had written since Franz Schubert, the great Austrian composer who died in 1828. Among Schumann's other chief works for piano are *Symphonic Etudes* (1834), *Fantasia in C Major* (1836), and *Concerto in A Minor* (1845). He composed a number of shorter pieces and composed four symphonies, chamber and choral music, and many string quartets. His collection of pieces for piano students, *Album for the Young*, was published in 1848. Indeed, Schumann's compositions represent two contrasting moods of romantic music, one emotional and volatile, and the other quiet and introspective.

As the years of productivity and happiness progressed, Schumann began to show signs of mental illness. He suffered a severe breakdown in the winter of 1842-43, and had to relinquish the position as editor of his music journal. In 1850, he accepted the position of musical director of the Düsseldorf symphony orchestra, but because of difficulties associated with his mental illness he was forced to resign in 1853. Sometime later, Schumann was placed in an asylum where he spent the remaining two years of his life. He died there on July 29, 1856.

Robert Schumann wrote many musical compositions and critiques for his journal, praising the works of other composers and musicians. He loved young people and some of his best work—*Kinderscenen* (*Scenes from Childhood*) and *Album for Children*—is devoted to children all over the world.

Name _____

Robert Schumann

MATERIALS: Paper, pen, a Robert Schumann recording.

ACTIVITY:

1. Robert Schumann was a superb composer. Like him, you will compose lyrics for a musical piece. Choose a song that has no words.

2. This will be a challenge, but think of words that fit the sound you hear. The song, for example, might be about a special place or event.

3. Take the time to listen to the music as many times as you want. Sing along with the music after you have completed your lyrics.

Evaluation   Name _____

THINKING ABOUT ROBERT SCHUMANN AND ME

Respond to four or more of the following questions/statements:

1. Explain the process or steps taken to write your song. How did you get your idea? How long did it take you? Was it difficult or easy?

2. Schumann injured one of his fingers and had to give up the piano. This did not hurt his career because he took up composing instead. Did you ever have to give up something you loved? What happened when you did? Did anything good come of it? Explain.

3. Schumann first studied law before he switched to music. Do you have a dream that you would like to follow? What is it?

4. The end of Schumann's life was very sad. Explain in your own words what happened to him and why it was so sad.

5. What other famous musicians were good friends with the Schumann family? Why is it important for people in the same field or career to be friends?

6. Write one or more paragraphs about what you have learned about this composer and/or what you have learned through your activity project relating to this composer.

Piotr Ilyich Tchaikovsky (chi-kawf-skee) 1840–1893

Piotr Ilyich Tchaikovsky was the first Russian composer to gain international fame. His music was melancholy, spirited, lyrical, and lively—it was universal music. A master of orchestration, Tchaikovsky also possessed a gift for melody. He composed many songs, eleven operas, ballet music, various types of orchestral works, and chamber music. Tchaikovsky is most famous for his six symphonies, particularly *Symphony No. 4* (1877), *Symphony No. 5* (1888), and *Symphony No. 6* (also called *Pathétique*), written in 1893.

Piotr Ilyich was born into a well-to-do and music-loving family on May 7, 1840, in Kamsko-Votkinsk, Russia. He began taking piano lessons when he was four years old and continued to play until he was ten. When Piotr was ten years old, he was sent to study the principles of law at a school in St. Petersburg (now Leningrad). While Piotr's musical talent pleased his family, his parents did not foresee a musical career for him. So unlike any other famous composer, Piotr grew up without seriously studying music. Young Piotr continued to study at the law school until he was nineteen, then he became a clerk in the Ministry of Justice. He had little time to devote to music but it remained foremost in his mind. After failing to secure an appointment to a higher position in the Ministry of Justice, Piotr decided to dedicate his life to music.

From 1862 to 1866, Tchaikovsky studied music at the St. Petersburg Conservatory under Anton Rubenstein, a pianist and composer. During this time he supported himself by giving music lessons. From 1866 to 1877, Tchaikovsky taught harmony at the Moscow Conservatory and began work on his first symphony and an opera.

When he was twenty-eight years old, Tchaikovsky met the "Famous Five" in St. Petersburg. This group of young Russian composers consisted of Balakirev, the founder of the group who later became very important to Tchaikovsky's musical development; Cui; Borodin; Mussorgsky; and Rimsky-Korsakov. But the composers who influenced Tchaikovsky the most were Wolfgang Amadeus Mozart, a miraculous eighteenth century Austrian; and Mikhail Glinka, a

Russian composer who died in 1857 and is most famous for his opera *Russlan and Ludmilla*.

Tchaikovsky was a shy man, but he decided to marry in 1877. The marriage was brief, and when he and his wife separated within a few weeks, Tchaikovsky came close to a nervous breakdown. He suffered other discouraging setbacks in his career as well, but fortunately, the power and passion of music was strong enough to raise him up from these defeats. Gradually, Tchaikovsky's music became recognized and he traveled to Italy, Germany, and Switzerland as an accomplished composer.

In 1876, one of Tchaikovsky's pupils introduced him by letter to Nadezhda von Meck, a wealthy woman who greatly admired Tchaikovsky's music. At first von Meck asked Tchaikovsky to arrange piano transcriptions of his music for her. Then she asked his permission to give him enough money every year so that he could give up teaching and devote all his time to composition. She insisted that they never meet, though they exchanged letters for years. Madame von Meck's generous financial support undoubtedly helped Tchaikovsky to regain his strength and compose his finest music. He left the Moscow Conservatory, concentrated on composing, and traveled widely.

In 1891, Tchaikovsky took part in the opening of Carnegie Hall in New York City where he conducted a concert at the dedication ceremony. The following year Tchaikovsky's famous ballet, *The Nutcracker*, was presented for the first time. Tchaikovsky's three ballets—*Swan Lake* (1875–1876), *Sleeping Beauty* (1888-1889), and *The Nutcracker* (1892)—have become world-renowned classics. The concert version of *The Nutcracker*, *The Nutcracker Suite*, remains the most famous and best-loved of Tchaikovsky's compositions.

In 1893, Tchaikovsky visited London where he was honored with a doctorate from Cambridge University. In October of that year he conducted the first of his six symphonies, *Pathétique*, at St. Petersburg.

Along with his masterful symphonies and beautiful, expressive ballets, Tchaikovsky's lyrical *Romeo and Juliet Overture*; the *1812 Overture* for the Moscow Exhibition; the symphonic poem *Manfred*; the orchestral work *Italian Capriccio*; and the operas *Eugene Onégin* and *Queen of Spades*, based on the works of the Russian poet Alexander Pushkin; all stand as in immortal tribute to Russia's most celebrated composer.

Activity Sheet   Name _____

Piotr Ilyich Tchaikovsky

MATERIALS: Musical story paper on the following page, crayons or markers, pencil.

ACTIVITY:

1. Compose music for a published story or for your own original story. Then illustrate your musical story. Use as many sheets of music story paper as you want.

2. Share your musical story with friends and relatives.

MUSICAL STORY PAPER

Evaluation   Name _____

THINKING ABOUT TCHAIKOVSKY AND ME

Respond to four or more of the following questions/statements:

1. Tchaikovsky traveled to Italy, Germany, and Switzerland as an accomplished composer. Locate these countries on a map. Then list three countries where you would like to travel. Explain why you chose the countries you did.

2. Who were the two composers that influenced Tchaikovsky the most?

3. Choose 3–6 toys to come alive for a ballet. Which toys did you choose? Why?

4. When Tchaikovsky studied at the St. Petersburg Conservatory, he supported himself by giving music lessons. If you were studying for a specific career, what would it be? How would you support yourself?

5. Write the name of one of Tchaikovsky's musical compositions. Then write how this music makes you feel and what you think about as you listen to it.

6. Write one or more paragraphs about what you have learned about this composer and/or what you have learned through your activity project relating to this composer.

Antonio Vivaldi
(vih–vahl–dee)
1678–1741

Antonio Vivaldi, an Italian composer from Venice, was the master of the concerto. A concerto is a instrumental composition in which the orchestra accompanies one or more solo instruments. Vivaldi wrote in a variety of musical styles: concertos, operas, symphonies, sonatas, and sacred compositions. As one of the most productive composers of baroque music, Vivaldi helped develop the baroque concerto. During Vivaldi's lifetime, many famous composers, including Johann Sebastian Bach, studied Vivaldi's concertos. Like Vivaldi's compositions, Bach's music was forgotten shortly after his death. Many, many years later, long after both Vivaldi and Bach had died, other musicians rediscovered their music and there emerged new and enthusiastic support for the forgotton composers. Since then, both men's music is heard all over the world and they are considered among the greatest composers known to humankind. Some of Vivaldi's most well-known concertos are *The Four Seasons*, *The Night*, *The Hunt*, and *Storm at Sea*.

Antonio Vivaldi was born in Venice, Italy, in 1678. Vivaldi was fortunate to have been born in such a culturally active city, but he was also fortunate to have the name "Vivaldi," a famous and much admired name throughout Italy.

Antonio Vivaldi's father was a violinist at the Ducal Palace of San Marco and it was he who taught Antonio to play the violin when he was just a young boy. Antonio's father wanted Antonio to succeed him as the musician of the family rather than Antonio's two brothers, who were in and out of trouble with the police.

When Antonio Vivaldi became an ordained priest in 1703, he was often called by his nickname, the Red Priest, because he had long, red hair. Vivaldi was appointed musical director at a school for female orphans and abandoned girls. The school where he taught and composed music was called the Ospedale della Piétà. There Vivaldi wrote numerous cantatas (vocal works—choruses, solos, and duets—accompanied by musical instruments) and concertos which were performed in a public concert by the schoolgirls each Sunday. Vivaldi's best known sacred choral composition is *Gloria in D Major* (1708).

Vivaldi's students worked and studied passionately. When these young girls performed in public they were hidden behind a grille because people assumed the girls were deformed in some way. Vivaldi had a very demanding job. In addition to composing and playing for the Ospedale della Piéta, he was also in charge of caring for all the instruments there. And because he was such a skilled violinist and talented composer and many wealthy families in Venice wanted his music to accompany their special celebrations, he was kept hard at work, furnishing new scores. Vivaldi continually experimented with new styles; he would compose for an oboe one day, and for a flute the next. At one point, Antonio was writing an opera a day. His contemporaries marveled at the speed at which he could write such lively, colorful compositions.

Vivaldi's most famous work was entitled *The Battle of Harmony and Invention* from which stems the famous concerti *The Four Seasons*. In *The Four Seasons*, we hear sounds imitate the chirping of birds to signify spring, and harsh howling winds to signify winter. In this regard, Vivaldi's music is "programmatic." Vivaldi was one of the first composers to write "program" music—long before the composers Franz Liszt or Richard Strauss, who were both nineteenth century composers.

Vivaldi traveled widely, often to Prague, Vienna, and Amsterdam (where his music was published) to conduct his own works. A long sufferer of asthma, Vivaldi returned to Vienna where he died in July of 1741. The "Red Priest's" fine music still greatly enriches our world today and serves as inspiration to all his students and listeners.

Antonio Vivaldi

MATERIALS: 22" x 28" sheet of colored posterboard, scissors, and a Vivaldi recording.

ACTIVITY:

1. Antonio Vivaldi learned to play the violin beautifully. You will pretend to be Vivaldi.

2. With the full sheet of colored posterboard, draw a violin. Refer to the illustration above for help. Once you have drawn your violin, cut it out. Put strings on your violin as seen in the illustration above.

3. Save the posterboard scrap to make a bow for your violin.

4. For fun, play your violin along with a Vivaldi recording.

Evaluation   Name _____

THINKING ABOUT VIVALDI AND ME

Respond to four or more of the following questions/statements:

1. Antonio Vivaldi had two careers at the same time. What were they? Could you successfully pursue two different careers at the same time? Explain.

2. Vivaldi's father chose Antonio to be the family musician and taught him how to play the violin. What family member or friend has taught you something special, such as how to prepare a favorite meal or play a fun game?

3. Vivaldi had a nickname. What was it? Do you or your friends have nicknames? What are they and how did the nicknames get started?

4. Why do you think Bach, the eighteenth century composer, rearranged Vivaldi's music?

5. How did your violin turn out? Describe the most difficult and/or most fun part about creating your violin. Do you think you would ever like to play a real violin? Why or why not?

6. Write one or more paragraphs about what you have learned about this composer and/or what you have learned through your activity project relating to this composer.

ENRICHMENT OR SUBSTITUTE ACTIVITIES

Study photos and/or statues of composers. Then make a sculpture of a composer from clay.

Read as much as possible about a specific composer. Then write a play about this person's life.

Study a specific composer. Then make a time line of important dates in his/her life.

Read as much as possible about a composer. Then make a map (or web) about the things that this person did to become famous.

Make a crossword puzzle that relates to music. For example, you might want to create a puzzle using names of musical instruments and musical terms.

Make a collage of musical items on a large sheet of paper.

Illustrate and label as many instruments as you can think of on a large sheet of paper.

Make a musical alphabet book. Write each letter of the alphabet on a separate sheet of paper and staple these together to make a booklet. Then draw pictures that relate to music on the proper pages. For the letter "A" page, for example, you might draw and "accordion" and/or an "audience" on it. (*Note:* Some letters you may have to leave blank.)

Look at portraits of composers. Then make a pointillism (painting or drawing with small dots) portrait of one of your favorite composers.

Read some poetry. Then write music for a favorite poem.

Be a composer! Create and write music and lyrics of your own.

Name _____

MUSICAL GROUPS

List at least six instruments under each of the proper headings.

BRASS INSTRUMENTS

1) _____   5) _____

2) _____   6) _____

3) _____   7) _____

4) _____   8) _____

PERCUSSION INSTRUMENTS

1) _____   5) _____

2) _____   6) _____

3) _____   7) _____

4) _____   8) _____

STRING INSTRUMENTS

1) _____   5) _____

2) _____   6) _____

3) _____   7) _____

4) _____   8) _____

WOODWINDS

1) _____   5) _____

2) _____   6) _____

3) _____   7) _____

4) _____   8) _____

Name_____

CREATIVE MUSIC PROJECT
(FOR INDEPENDENT LEARNING)

MATERIALS NEEDED:_____

_____

_____

PLANS FOR MUSIC PROJECT: _____

_____

_____

_____

ADULT APPROVAL

Did you have any problems in creating your project? Why or why not?

What did you learn from creating this project that will help you do better on your next project?

Make a sketch of your finished project and write a brief description of it.

Name _____

NOTES ABOUT COMPOSERS

Write a riddle about a composer on the front of the note and write the answer to the riddle on the back of it. Then put each note that you make on a musical staff bulletin board.

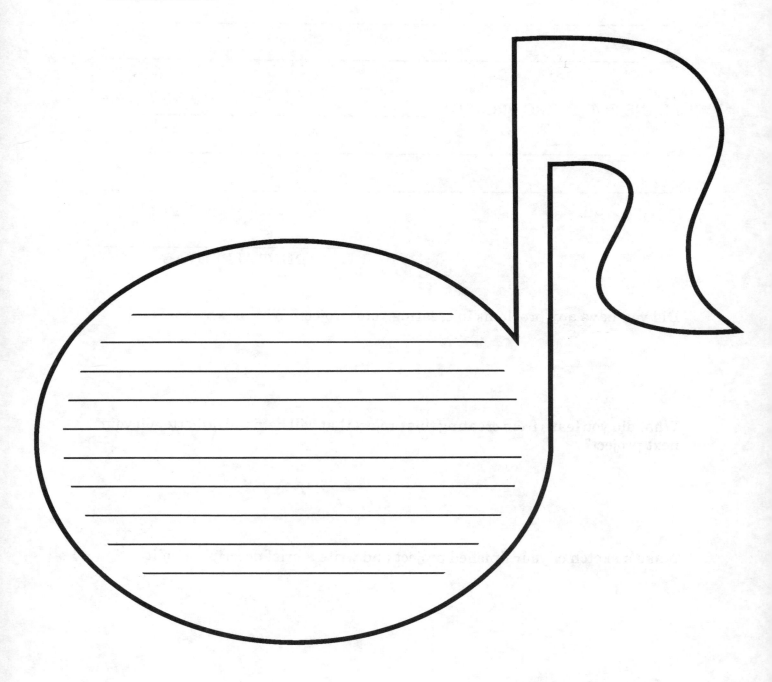

Name_____

MUSICAL DICTIONARY

MATERIALS: A paper booklet with one page for each letter of the alphabet; crayons, markers, or colored pencils; and a pencil.

ACTIVITY:

1. Write each alphabet letter on a separate page of the booklet.

2. Then draw musical objects or terms that begin with that letter on each of the pages to make a musical dictionary.

GLOSSARY

accompaniment—a vocal or instrumental part that supports a solo part.

acrostic poem—a poem that is made out of the shape of the word that the poem is about.

baroque music—occurring between the years 1600–1750; baroque music is characterized by an elaborate style, grand effects, and highly ornamented details.

beat—the audible, visual, or mental marking of divisions in music.

bow—a rod with horsehair drawn tightly between its ends. When the bow is dragged over a stringed instrument, the instrument produces sound.

cantata—a work for solo voice or voices and chorus, often with orchestral accompaniment.

capel maestro (or **capelmeister**)—the conductor or teacher in a church choir.

chamber music—instrumental music for a small group of musicians with each musician playing a solo part; this music is intended for a small audience.

chorale—a term used before the nineteenth century to describe a song that praised God; "chorale" also describes a group of singers.

choreograph—to design or create dance steps to go along with music.

classical music—occurring between the years 1750–1825; classical music stresses balance, clarity, and order, and stimulates the intellect or mind.

clavichord—an early keyboard instrument producing soft sounds.

clavier—any musical instrument (other than an organ) having a keyboard; such as a clavichord, harpsichord, or piano.

concertino—a short concerto.

concerto—a musical composition, generally in three movements, for one or more principal solo instruments and orchestra.

conductor—the leader, guide, or director of an orchestra or chorus who communicates interpretation of the music to the performers by using his/her baton or hands.

convention—a traditional standard or custom.

copyright—a form of protection put on creative works so no one else can copy or borrow the works and claim credit for them.

creative—having original, imaginative, and productive thought and expressions.

critic—a person who judges, evaluates, or reviews literary or artistic works, or musical or dramatic performances.

critique—to view or listen to a work of art and then discuss the work's strengths and weaknesses. It is a form of criticism that evaluates both the merits and faults in a work.

cue—a sign, signal, or clue to prompt someone or something to action.

development—the second movement in sonata form that takes the original theme and adds more details and ideas. It can even stray away from the original idea.

dynamics—in music, the high and low volume areas that will give a musical composition drama and interest.

exposition—the first movement in sonata form that exposes or tells the main theme of the music.

folk music—music which originated among the common people of a nation or region and is usually passed on from one generation to another.

fugue—a musical composition usually in three parts (exposition, development, and recapitulation) and written in three, four, or five voice parts; the first melody is continually repeated and imitated throughout the entire piece.

genius—a person who possesses an extremely high amount of intelligence.

harpsichord—a keyboard instrument in common use between the sixteenth to the eighteenth century, before the birth of the piano. The harpsichord has a more delicate tone.

improvise—to make up or create while singing or playing without an initial plan.

journalist—a person who reports, writes, edits, or photographs news as a business or occupation.

largo—a musical term signaling slowness in a broad, dignified style.

lyrics—the words that go along with the music in a song.

masquerade—a party where all of the guests and the hosts wear masks and/or costumes to disguise themselves.

Mass—the principal practice of the Roman Catholic Church; originally the Mass was intended for the unaccompanied chorus, but has subsequently been performed with solo voices and orchestra as well. A popular form among Romantic and modern composers.

mazurkas—a lively and quick Polish dance, or music for this particular dance.

melody—an organized sequence of single tones arranged to make up a musical phrase or idea.

nocturne—dreamy, "nighttime" music, usually from the romantic period and composed for the piano.

octet—a musical piece created for eight performers, or a group of eight performers who play music together.

opera—like a play, but the words are sung on stage while an orchestra plays the music.

oratorio—an extended musical composition based upon a biblical text for solo voices, chorus, and orchestra.

orchestra—an instrumental group consisting of string, wind, brass, and percussion instruments. (Examples: string—violin, wind—clarinet, brass—French horn, percussion—cymbals.)

orchestration—to arrange or compose music for performance by an orchestra.

organ—a musical instrument consisting of one or more sets of pipes and one or more keyboards capable of producing a wide range of musical effects when supplied with air.

overture—a single movement or piece of music that introduces an opera, play, or oratario.

polonaise—a dignified dance of Polish heritage that is done quickly or in triple time.

portrait—a painting, drawing, or photograph conveying a likeness of a person (or family), especially the face(s).

programmatic music—music that attempts to describe a landscape, an event, a place, or a feeling.

prodigy—in reference to Mozart, a prodigy is one who shows superb skill at something, like playing an instrument or composing, without having been properly trained.

pursue—to try to get or achieve something.

quintet—a musical piece created for five performers, or a group of five performers who play music together.

recapitulation—the third movement in a sonata form. It is the return to the original theme of the music and ties or connects the musical themes together.

recital—when one or two musicians perform their talents.

renaissance—music during the time period of 1450–1600 that sprung from ideas of the revival of human interests and cultural values such as art, science, architecture, and religion.

requiem—a Mass for the dead which uses the text of the Mass without the *Gloria* and *Credo* sections.

romantic music—occurring between the years 1825–1900; romantic music emphasizes free expression of imagination and emotion with emphasis on the melody.

royalty—a payment an artist receives from a company that has purchased and published his/her work. The payment usually comes once a year for musicians and authors.

sonata—an instrumental work including three or four movements or parts that are played one after the other and are related to each other (for either solo piano or for an instrument and piano). Usually the first movement of a symphony is in sonata form.

sonata form—a form in the first movement of a symphony that consists of three movements: the exposition, the development, and the recapitulation.

sonatina—a short sonata.

string quartet—a musical composition, usually in four movements, for four stringed instruments (usually two violins, a viola, and a cello).

stringed instrument—an instrument, such as a violin, that gets its sound from stretched string.

symphony—a large instrumental work for an orchestra.

technique—the manner and ability in which a skill is accomplished.

tempo—the rate, rhythm, or pattern of movement in music.

texture—in a musical composition, texture refers to the arrangement and quality of various parts and the feelings they may arouse. The music may be smooth and flowing, or fast and choppy.

virtuoso—in music, a highly skilled musician who is very talented and displays brilliant technique when playing an instrument or composing music.

COMPOSER BIBLIOGRAPHY

JOHANN SEBASTIAN BACH

Barber, David W. *Bach, Beethoven, and the Boys*. Illustrated by Dave Donald. Toronto: Sound and Vision, 1986.

Brownell, David. *Great Composers (Bach to Berlioz)*. Illustrated by Nancy Conkle. Santa Barbara, CA: Bellerophon Books, 1985.

Millar, Cynthia. *Bach and His World* (Great Masters Series). Morristown, NJ: Silver Burdett, 1980.

Palmer, Willard A. (Editor). *J.S. Bach (An Introduction to His Keyboard Music)*. Van Nuys, CA: Alfred Publishing Company, MCMLXXIII.

Ventura, Piero. *Great Composers*. New York: G.P. Putman's Sons, 1989.

LUDWIG VAN BEETHOVEN

Barber, David W. *Bach, Beethoven, and the Boys*. Illustrated by Dave Donald. Toronto: Sound and Vision, 1986.

Greene, Carol *Ludwig Van Beethoven (Musical Pioneer)*. Chicago: Childrens Press, 1989.

Palmer, Willard A. (Editor). *Beethoven (An Introduction to His Piano Works)*. Van Nuys, CA: Alfred Publishing Company, MCMLXX.

Thompson, Wendy. *Ludwig Van Beethoven (Composer's World)*. New York: Viking, 1990.

LEONARD BERNSTEIN

Boughton, Simon. *Great Lives*. New York: Doubleday, 1988.

Cone, Molly. *Leonard Bernstein*. Illustrations by Robert Galster. New York: Thomas Y. Crowell, 1970. (picture book)

Reidy, John P. and Norman Richards. *Leonard Bernstein* (People of Destiny Series). Chicago: Childrens Press, 1967.

Tomb, Eric. *American Composers*. Illustrations by Nancy Conkle. Santa Barbara, CA: Bellerophon Books, 1991.

JOHANNES BRAHMS

Boughton, Simon. *Great Lives*. New York: Doubleday, 1988.

Brownell, David; Nancy Conkle, Eric Tomb, and Paul Rail. *Great Composers (Chopin to Tchaikovsky)*. Santa Barbara, CA: Bellerophon Books, 1989.

Bye, Lean L. *Student's Guide to the Great Composers (A Guide to Music History for Students)*. Pacific, MO: Bayside Press, 1988.

Ventura, Piero. *Great Composers*. New York: G.P. Putnam's Sons, 1989.

FREDERIC CHOPIN

Brownell, David; Nancy Conkle, Eric Tomb, and Paul Rail. *Great Composers (Chopin to Tchaikovsky)*. Santa Barbara, CA: Bellerophon Books, 1989.

Bye, Dean L. *Student's Guide to the Great Composers*. Pacific, MO: Bayside Press, 1988.

Palmer, Willard A. (Editor). *Chopin (An Introduction to His Piano Works)*. Van Nuys, CA: Alfred Publishing Company, MCMLXXI.

Ventura, Piero. *Great Composers*. New York: G.P. Putnan's Sons, 1989.

DUKE ELLINGTON

Boughton, Simon. *Great Lives*. New York: Doubleday, 1988.

Frankl, Ron. *Duke Ellington*. New York: Chelsea House, 1986.

Barclay, Pamela. *Duke Ellington (Ambassador of Music)*. Illustrations by Harold Henriksen. Mankato, MN: Creative Education, 1974.

Ventura, Piero. *Great Composers*. New York: G.P. Putnam's Sons, 1989.

GEORGE GERSHWIN

Bye, Dean L. *Student's Guide to the Great Composers*. Some illustrations by Barb Kimker-Furry. Pacific, MO: Bayside Press, 1988.

Michell, Barbara. *America, I Hear You (A Story About George Gershwin)*. Illustrated by Jan Hosking Smith. Minneapolis: Carolrhoda, 1987.

Tomb, Eric. *American Composers*. Illustrations by Nancy Conkle. Santa Barbara, CA: Bellerophon Books, 1991.

Ventura, Piero. *Great Composers*. New York: Putnam's Sons, 1989.

GEORGE FREDERICK HANDEL

Brownell, David. *Great Composers (Bach to Berlioz)*. Illustrated by Nancy Conkle. Santa Barbara, CA: Bellerophon Books, 1985.

Bye, Dean L. *Student's Guide to the Great Composers*. Pacific, MO: Bayside Press, 1988.

Lucktenberg, George (Editor). *Handel (An Introduction to His Keyboard Works)*. Van Nuys, CA: Alfred Publishing Company, MCMLXXV.

Stevens, Bryna. *Handel (And the Famous Sword Swallower of Halle)*. Illustrated by Ruth Tietjen Councell. New York: Philomel Books, 1990. (picture book)

FRANZ JOSEPH HAYDN

Barbers, David W. *Bach, Beethoven, and the Boys*. Illustrations by Dave Donald. Toronto: Sound and Vision, 1986.

Bouthton, Simon. *Great Lives*. New York: Doubleday, 1988.

Brownell, David. *Great Composesrs (Bach to Berlioz)*. Illustrated by Nancy Conkle. Santa Barbara, CA: Bellerophon Books, 1985.

Bye, Dean L. *Student's Guide to the Great Composers*. Some illustrations by Barb Kimker-Furry. Pacific, MO: Bayside Press, 1988.

Ventura, Piero. *Great Composers*. New York: G.P. Putman's Sons, 1989.

FANNY MENDELSSOHN

Plantamura, Carol. *Woman Composers*. Santa Barbara, CA: Bellerophon Books, 1985.

FELIX MENDELSSOHN

Brownell, David. *Great Composers (Bach to Berlioz)*. Illustrations by Nancy Conkle. Santa Barbara, CA. Bellerophon Books, 1985.

Bye, Dean L. *Students Guide to the Great Composers*. Some illustrations by Barb Kimker-Furry. Pacific, MO: Bayside Press, 1988.

Halford, Margery (Editor). *Mendelssohn (An Introduction To His Piano Works)*. Van Nuys, CA: Alfred Publishing Company, MCMLXXVII.

Ventura, Piero. *Great Composers*. New York: G.P. Putman's Sons, 1989.

WOLFGANG AMADEUS MOZART

Brighton, Catherine. *Mozart (Scenes from the Childhood of the Great Composer.* New York: Doubleday, 1990. (picture book)

Downing, Julie. *Mozart Tonight.* New York: Bradbury, 1991. (picture book).

Green, Carol. *Wolfgang Amadeus Mozart: Musician*: Chicago: Childrens Press, 1987.

Palmer, Willard A (Editor). *W.A. Mozart* (An Introduction to his Keyboard Works). Van Nuys, CA: Alfred Publishing Company, 1974.

Thompson, Wendy. *Wolfgang Amedeus Mozart* (Composer's World Series). New York: 1990.

COLE PORTER

Boughton, Simon. *Great Lives.* New York: Doubleday, 1988.

Porter, Cole. *The Best of Cole Porter* (E-Z Play Today for organs, pianos, and electronic keyboards). Milwaukee, WI: Hal Leonard Publishing Corporation, 1975.

Salsini, Paul. *Cole Porter: Twentieth Century Composer of Popular Songs.* Charlotteville, NY: Sam Har Press, 1972.

SERGEI SERGEIVITCH PROKOFIEV

Boughton, Simon. *Great Lives.* New York: Doubleday, 1988.

Herring, Ann King. *S.S. Prokovfiev's Peter and the Wolf.* Illustrated by Kozo Shimizu. Tokyo: Gakken Company, 1971.

Prokofiev, Sergei. *Peter and the Wolf.* Illustrations by Jorg Muller. New York: Alfred A. Knopf. (A picture book and cassette.)

FRANZ SCHUBERT

Boughton, Simon. *Great Lives.* New York: Doubleday, 1988.

Brownell, David. *Great Composers (Bach to Berlioz).* Illustrations by Nancy Conkle. Santa Barbara, CA: Bellerophon Books, 1985.

Bye Dean L. *Student's Guide to the Great Composers.* Some illustrations by Barb Kimker-Furry. Pacific, MO: Bayside Press, 1988.

Ventura, Piero. *Great Composers.* New York: G.P. Putnam's Sons, 1989.

CLARA SCHUMANN

Plantamura, Carol. *Women Composers*. Santa Barbara, CA: Bellerophon Books, 1985.

Reich, Nancy B. *Clara Schumann. (The Artist and the Woman)*. New York: Cornell University, 1985. (Adult Book.)

ROBERT SCHUMANN

Brownell, David; Nancy Conkle, Eric Tomb, and Paul Rail. *Great Composers (Chopin to Tchaikovsky)*. Santa Barbara: Bellerophon Books, 1989.

Bouthton, Simon. *Great Lives*. New York: Doubleday, 1988.

Ventura, Piero. *Great Composers*. New York: Putman's Sons, 1989.

PETER TCHAIKOVSKY

Brownell, David; Nancy Conkle, Eric Tomb, and Paul Rail. *Great Composers (Chopin to Tchaikovsky)*. Santa Barbara, CA: Bellerophon Books, 1989.

Herring, Ann King. *P.I. Tchaikovsky's—The Nutcracker*. Illustrated by Fumiko Hori. Adapted by Magoichi Kushida. Tokyo: Gakken Company, 1971.

Storr, Catherine (retold). *The Nutcracker* (Easy Piano Picture Book). Illustrated by Dianne Jackson. London: Faber and Faber, 1987.

Ventura, Piero. *Great Composers*. New York: G.P. Putman's Sons, 1989.

ANTONIO VIVALDI

Bouthton, Simon. *Great Lives*, New York: Doubleday, 1988.

Ventura, Piero. *Great Composers*. New York: G.P. Putman's Sons, 1989.

ABOUT THE AUTHORS

HARRIET KINGHORN

Harriet Kinghorn has taught preschool, kindergarten, grades two through four, and the Enrichment Program in East Grand Forks, Minnesota. She holds a Bachelor of Science and Master of Science in Education. Harriet has had a number of items published in various educational magazines. She has also authored and co-authored numerous activity books, including *Independent Activities* (Grades 1–6) with Dale Taylor, *Storytime Patterns* with Robert King, and *Let's Meet Famous Artists* with Jacqueline Badman and Lisa Lewis-Spicer. Harriet was honored as one of twelve "Honor Teachers of Minnesota" in 1976. Harriet presently lives in Fort Collins, Colorado, where she is creating and writing full time.

JACQUELINE BADMAN

Jacqueline Badman lives in Grand Forks, North Dakota, with her husband David. She works full time for the University of North Dakota's Division of Continuing Education as the Program Coordinator for the "Learning After Hours Programs." She is also presently pursuing a Master's of Science Degree in Adult Education. With a Bachelor of Fine Arts and graduate study in painting and drawing, Jacqueline is very interested in educating children and adults in the Fine Arts. This is the second book Jacqueline has co-authored with Harriet Kinghorn and Lisa Lewis-Spicer.

LISA LEWIS-SPICER

Lisa Lewis-Spicer received her Master of Arts in English from the University of North Dakota where she has been a lecturer for seven years, specializing in writing classes centered on *The New Yorker* magazine. Lisa lives in Grand Forks, North Dakota, with her husband, four children, and two cats—they all enjoy listening and dancing to a wide variety of music.

BIBLIOGRAPHY: CASSETTES

Bach: His Story and His Music. New York: Moss Music Group.

Mr. Bach Comes to Call. New York: Classical Kids.

Beethoven Lives Upstairs. New York: Classical Kids.

Chopin: His Story and His Music. New York: Moss Music Group.

Handel: His Story and His Music. New York: Moss Music Group.

Haydn: His Story and His Music. New York: Moss Music Group.

Mendelssohn: His Story and His Music. New York: Moss Music Group.

Mozart: His Story and His Music. New York: Moss Music Group.

Mozart's "Magic Flute." New York: Classical Kids.

Schubert: His Story and His Music. New York: Moss Music Group.

Vivaldi and Corelli: Their Stories and Their Music. New York: Moss Music Group.

TEACHER'S NOTES

TEACHER'S NOTES

TEACHER'S NOTES

TEACHER'S NOTES